POCKET VENICE

TOP EXPERIENCES • LOCAL LIFE

HELENA SMITH, ABIGAIL BLASI

Contents

Gondolas
LEOKS/SHUTTERSTOCK ©

Explore Venice 37

Survival Guide 173

Special Features

Welcome to Venice

'Ooooooeeeee!', gondoliers call out in narrow canals. With the world's highest density of Unesco-protected masterpieces, Venice will make you cry out too. Once you've seen palaces built on water, partied like Casanova in costume and eaten chorus lines of red-footed lagoon scallops, you'll greet every canal bend with anticipation.

People in Carnevale (p18) costumes and masks
FOTOGRAFICHE/SHUTTERSTOCK ©

Top Experiences

Marvel at Dome Mosaics at Basilica di San Marco (p40)

BORYANA MANZUROVA/SHUTTERSTOCK ©

Indulge in History at Palazzo Ducale (p44)

PAVEL TVRDY/SHUTTERSTOCK ©

Go Gothic at I Frari (p92)

CHRISTIAN MUELLER/SHUTTERSTOCK ©

Find Fresh Food at Rialto Market (p94)

Tour Tintoretto at Scuola Grande di San Rocco (p90)

SHUSTRIKS/SHUTTERSTOCK ©

LUCAMATO/SHUTTERSTOCK ©

Admire Art at Gallerie dell' Accademia (p68)

Visit the Palatial Peggy Guggenheim Collection (p72)

Explore Campo del Ghetto Nuovo & the Ghetto (p118)

OLEG ZNAMENSKIY/SHUTTERSTOCK ©

ALBERTO MASNOVO/SHUTTERSTOCK ©

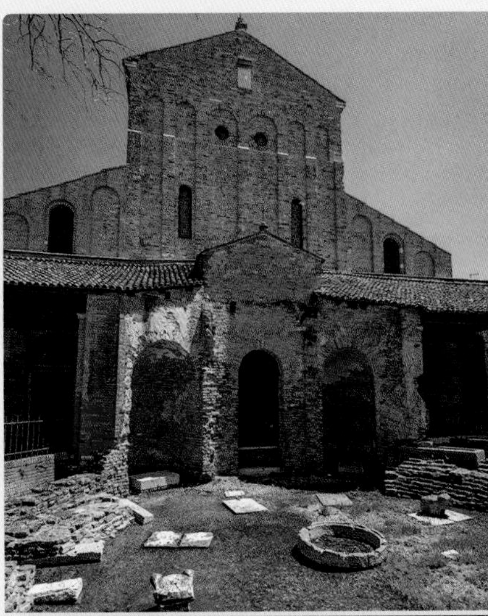

Gaze at Byzantine Splendour in Torcello (p164)

Savour the View from Basilica di San Giorgio Maggiore (p152)

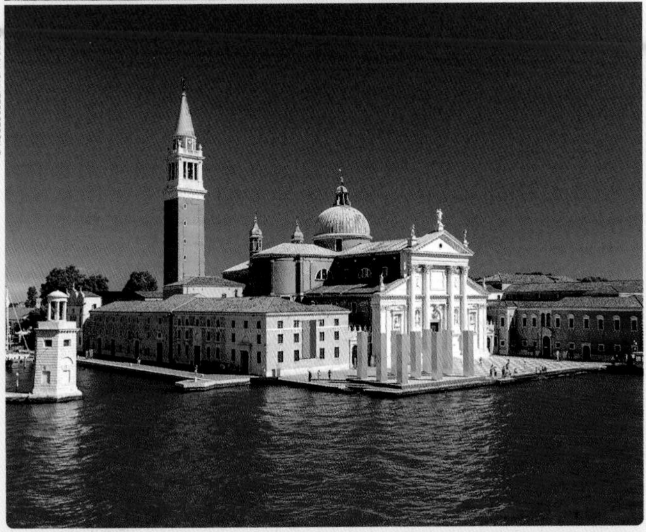

SCSTOCK/SHUTTERSTOCK ©

Dining Out

The visual blitz that is Venice can leave visitors weak-kneed and grasping for the nearest panino *(sandwich). But there's more to La Serenissima than simple carb-loading. For centuries Venice has lavished visitors with inventive feasts. Now it's your turn to devour addictive* cicheti *(Venetian tapas) and a lagoon's worth of succulent seafood.*

Venetian Cuisine

Cross-cultural fusion food is old news here: 13th-century Venetian cookbooks include recipes for fish with galangal, saffron and ginger, a tradition that still inspires dishes at restaurants such as Bistrot de Venise (p57) and Osteria Trefanti (p106). Spice-route flavours feature in signature Venetian recipes such as *sarde in saor:* sardines in tangy onion marinade with pine nuts and sultanas.

Cicheti

Cicheti (pictured) are some of the best culinary finds in Italy, served at lunch and from around 6pm to 8pm. They range from basic bar snacks (spicy meatballs, tomato and basil bruschetta) to highly inventive small plates. Prices start at €1 for meatballs and range from €3 to €6 for gourmet *cicheti*.

Best Venetian Classics

Antiche Carampane Excellent seafood and moreish *fritto misto* (fried seafood) in Venice's former red-light corner (p106)

Trattoria Altanella Authentic Venetian recipes served up by the same family since 1920. (p159)

Da Codroma Venetian dishes accredited by Slow Food. (p80)

Trattoria al Gatto Nero Offers fabulous cooking, local ingredients and classic Venetian dishes. (p170)

Best Inventive Venetian

Venissa Osteria Sublime cooking with ingredients from the Lagoon and the surrounding fields. (p171)

CoVino A pocket-sized showcase for Slow Food produce. (p144)

Estro Gourmet *cicheti* and creative Venetian cooking. (p80)

TELSE/SHUTTERSTOCK ©

Best Cicheti

All'Arco Market-fresh morsels and zingy prosecco. (p106)

Ca' D'Oro alla Vedova Venice's most famous meatballs, sold in their hundreds from this historic favourite. (p121)

El Sbarlefo Local characters swing by this little wood-lined backstreet *cicheti* bar, whose name means 'the Smirk'. (p130)

Ostaria dai Zemei Creative concoctions from food-obsessed twins. (p107)

Best Vegan Venice

La Tecia Vegana Serious vegan food, with plant-based takes on Italian classics. (p81)

Suso Vegan ice-cream options. (p58)

Gelateria Il Doge More vegan ice-cream! (p75)

Peggy Guggenheim Collection The museum cafe serves daily vegan lunch specials including sweets. (p72)

Best Cheap Eats

Bar Ai Nomboli Inspired sandwiches and quality ingredients. (p107)

Pasticceria Tonolo The best pastry shop in Venice. (p80)

Al Mercà Lido restaurant in the former fish market, serving great *cicheti* and meals. (p155)

Cooking Course in Venice

If all that produce and tradition inspires the chef within, sign up for a Venetian cooking course. Acquolina Cooking School (p158) runs four- and eight-hour courses, the latter option including a morning trip to the Rialto Market. It also offers multiday courses, including accommodation.

Bar Open

When the siren sounds for acqua alta (high tide), Venetians close up shop and head home to put up their flood barriers – then pull on their boots and head right back out again. Why let floods disrupt a toast? It's not just a turn of phrase: come hell or high water, Venetians will find a way to have a good time.

What to Order

No rules seem to apply to drinking in Venice. No mixing spirits and wine? Venice's classic cocktails suggest otherwise; try a *spritz* (pictured), made with prosecco, soda water and bittersweet Aperol, bitter Campari or herbaceous Cynar. Price isn't an indicator of quality – you can pay €2.50 for a respectable *spritz*, or live to regret that €18 Bellini tomorrow (ouch). Don't be shy about asking fellow drinkers what they recommend; happy hour is a highly sociable affair.

DOC Versus IGT

In Italy, the official DOC *(denominazione d'origine controllata)* and elite DOCG (DOC *garantita* – guaranteed) designations are assurances of top-notch *vino* (wine). Yet, as successful as its wines are, the Veneto also bucks the DOC/DOCG system. Many of the region's small-production wineries can't be bothered with such external validation as they already sell out to Venetian bars and restaurants. As a result, some top producers prefer the IGT *(indicazione geografica tipica)* designation, which guarantees grapes typical of the region but leaves winemakers room to experiment.

Best Wine Bars

Vino Vero Natural, biodynamic and boutique drops in a standout Cannaregio wine bar. (p121)

Osteria ai Pugni Nightly canalside crowds and a changing choice of *vino* by the glass. (p83)

Al Timon Top-class wines by the glass and live music canalside. (p121)

Best for Beer

Birre da Tutto il Mondo o Quasi Venice's top beer bar

WEDDING AND LIFESTYLE/SHUTTERSTOCK ©

keeps punters purring with over 100 brews. (p131)

Il Santo Bevitore Trappist ales, seasonal stouts and football on TV. (p130)

Birreria Zanon A great place for a laid-back amber tipple from the craft beer selection. (p129)

Marciano Pub Canal views and craft beers from around the globe, including its own brew. (p130)

Best Signature Cocktails

Harry's Bar The driest classic in town is Harry's gin-heavy martini (no olive). (p60)

Locanda Cipriani Harry's famous white-peach Bellini tastes even better at Cipriani's island retreat. (p170)

Bar Longhi Drink top-class cocktails like orange martini in a jewel-like interior. (p59)

Bar Terrazza Danieli Apricot and orange moonlight with gin and grenadine. (p146)

Best Cafes

Grancaffè Quadri This baroque bar-cafe has been serving punters since 1699. (p59)

Torrefazione Cannaregio Veteran coffee roaster famed for hazelnut-laced espresso. (p130)

Caffè del Doge A serious selection of world coffees, including rare *kopi luwak*. (p110)

Coffee Tips

- In San Marco and other hot spots you can stand at the bar with the locals for a €1 to €2.50 coffee. To luxuriate inside a baroque cafe or idle in the outdoor seating, there's usually a €6 surcharge.
- Like your coffee milky but strong? Order a *macchiatone* rather than a cappuccino.

Treasure Hunt

Venice's best-kept secret: shopping. No illustrious shopping career is complete without trawling Venice for one-of-a-kind, artisan-made finds. All those souvenir tees and kitschy masks are nothing but decoys. Dig deeper and you'll stumble across the prized stuff – genuine, local and nothing short of inspiring.

Studio Visits

For your travelling companions who aren't sold on shopping, here's a convincing argument: in Venice, it really is an educational experience. In backstreet artisans' studios, you can watch ancient techniques used to make strikingly modern *carta memorizzata* (marbled paper) and Murano glass (pictured). Studios cluster together, so to find unique pieces, just wander key artisan areas: San Polo around Calle Seconda dei Saoneri; Santa Croce around Campo Santa Maria Mater Domini; San Marco along Frezzeria and Calle de la Botteghe; Dorsoduro around the Peggy Guggenheim Collection; Artisti Artigiani del Chiostro on Giudecca; and Murano.

DIY Souvenirs

Dodge the umpteen stalls selling plastic masks, and make your own authentic Venetian papier-mâché version at one of the workshops run by veteran mask maker Ca' Macana (p84). There are also mask-decorating workshops, with information on the history and meaning of these enigmatic, elegant creations.

Best Souvenirs

Pied à Terre Jewel-coloured *furlane* (gondolier slippers).

Gianni Basso Calling cards with the lion of San Marco. (p132)

Paolo Brandolisio Miniature *forcole* (carved gondola oarlocks). (p149)

Emilio Ceccato The official supplier of natty gondolier gear. (p114)

UNDERWORLD/SHUTTERSTOCK ©

Best Home Decor

Fortuny Tessuti Artistici Luxury, handmade textiles from an Italian style icon. (p161)

ElleElle Fetching sets of affordable hand-blown glass. (p167)

Chiarastella Cattana Sophisticated linens to restyle every corner of your *palazzo.* (p64)

DoppioFondo Original and striking images of Venice, hand-printed in-house. (p112)

Best Antiques

Claudia Canestrelli A walk-in curiosity cabinet with jewellery crafted from antique pieces. (p84)

Antichità al Ghetto A nostalgic mix of Venetian maps, art and jewellery. (p133)

Best Jewellery

Oh My Blue Cutting-edge creations from local and foreign designers. (p99)

Marina e Susanna Sent Striking, contemporary wearables good enough for MoMA. (p86)

Krumakata Striking, reasonably priced contemporary jewellery made from Murano glass. (p148)

Best Vintage Venice

L'Armadio di Coco Luxury Vintage Couture fashions of yesteryear at affordable prices. (p64)

Il Baule Blu Bag yourself a classic frock or some vintage Murano beads. (p114)

Tabarro San Marco Step back in time in a swirling woollen cloak, an icon of the city. (p99)

Best Leather Goods

Atelier Segalin di Daniela Ghezzo Custom-made shoes created with rare leather and seasoned style. (p64)

Balducci Borse Shoes and bags from a master leather craftsman. (p133)

Kalimala Natural tanning and top-shelf leather underline goods for men and women. (p148)

Show Time

No one throws a party like Venice, from Carnevale masquerades to Regata Storica floating parades and races. Year round you can hear live opera, baroque music and jazz, while the summer months see movie premieres and beach concerts. Many of the best events are casual pop-ups: keep your eyes peeled for posters and flyers around town.

Festivals

Carnevale (pictured) brings partying masqueraders on to the streets for the weeks preceding Lent. Tickets to La Fenice's masked balls run up to €250, but there are costume displays in every square and a Grand Canal flotilla to mark the start. From spring to November, the vast Biennale alternates contemporary art (even-numbered years) and architecture.

Venice International Film Festival runs from the last weekend in August through the first week of September, bringing together international star power and Italian fashion.

The city celebrates with November's Festa della Madonna della Salute and July's Festa del Redentore. Regatta season, from May's Vogalonga (p170) to early September's Regata Storica (www.regatastoricavenezia.it), sees furious boat races and partisan crowds.

Opera & Classical

You can still enjoy music as Venetians did centuries ago: Teatro La Fenice (p63) has been one of the world's top opera houses since 1792, while historical La Pietà (p147) orphanage is the original Vivaldi venue. Due to noise regulations in this small city with big echoes, shows typically end by 11pm.

Best Events

Carnevale (www.carnevale.venezia.it) Party in lavish costume through carnival season (about three weeks).

Venice Biennale Contemporary art and architecture in gorgeous pavilions. (p142)

Art Night Venezia (www.facebook.com/anv.artnightvenezia/) On a night in

SPARROWLENS/SHUTTERSTOCK ©

mid-June, galleries, shops and museums open late and showcase new artistic talent.

Venezia Jazz Festival (https://venetojazz.com/festival/venezia-jazz-festival/) Jazz greats and the odd pop star play historical venues in late June/early July.

Venice International Film Festival (www.labiennale.org/en/cinema/2022) Red carpets sizzle with star power in late August/early September, and deserving films actually win.

Venice Glass Week (www.theveniceglassweek.com) A week-long September festival celebrating over a thousand years of artisanship.

Best Live Music

Teatro La Fenice Divas hit new highs in this historical jewel-box theatre. (p63)

Palazetto Bru Zane Leading interpreters of Romantic music raise the Sebastiano Ricci–frescoed roof. (p111)

Musica a Palazzo Operatic dramas unfold in a Grand Canal palace, from receiving-room overtures to bedroom grand finales. (p49)

Venice Jazz Club Enjoy trad and Latin jazz at this canalside club. (p84)

Best Local Favourites

Laboratorio Occupato Morion (www.facebook.com/laboratorioccupatomorion) A radical backdrop for rocking regional bands.

Fondazione Giorgio Cini Occasionally serves up top-notch, modern world music. (p157)

Events Top Tips

- For upcoming events, see www.veneziaunica.it.
- During Carnevale book accommodation well in advance.
- In summer bars and beach clubs on the Lido host concerts and club nights.

Architecture

From glittering Byzantine churches to post-modern palaces, Venice astonishes at every turn. Its 1000-year architectural history has several high-water marks: pointy Gothic arches rounded off in the Renaissance; Palladio-revived classicism amid baroque flourishes; and stark modernism relaxing around decadent Lido Liberty (art nouveau).

Contemporary Venice

Despite the constraints of history, a surprising number of projects have turned Venice into a portfolio of contemporary architecture.

Architect Cino Zucchi kicked off the revival of Giudecca in 1995 with his conversion of 19th-century warehouses into art spaces and studio lofts. Since then, London firm David Chipperfield Architects has breathed new life into the cemetery island of San Michele. Meanwhile, rebirth of the artistic kind underscores Fondazione Giorgio Cini's redevelopment into a global cultural centre. Across the canal, Venice's historic Arsenale shipyards have been turned into Biennale art galleries; the striking Giardini pavilions by architects such as Alvar Aalto and Carlo Scarpa date to the 1950s.

In addition, French art collector François Pinault hired Japanese architect Tadao Ando to repurpose Palazzo Grassi and the Punta della Dogana into settings for his contemporary art collection, while Renzo Piano reinvented the Magazzini del Sale as a showcase for the Fondazione Vedova.

Culture and commerce co-exist in Dutch architect Rem Koolhaas' redevelopment of the Fondaco dei Tedeschi. Once a base for German merchants, the revamped 16th-century *palazzo* (mansion) now houses a department store and a publicly accessible rooftop.

Best Divine Architecture

Basilica di San Marco Byzantine domes glimmer with golden mosaics. (p40)

OLGAKHORKOVA/SHUTTERSTOCK ©

Basilica di Santa Maria della Salute Longhena's bubble-domed marvel, believed to have mystical curative powers. (p78)

Basilica di San Giorgio Maggiore Palladio's expansive, effortlessly uplifting church and cloisters. (p152)

I Frari A Gothic brick fancy with a scalloped roofline and a 14th-century *campanile* (bell tower). (p92)

Chiesa di Santa Maria dei Miracoli The Lombardos' little Renaissance miracle in polychrome marble. (p124)

Schola Spagnola The theatrical, elliptical women's gallery attributed to Longhena. (p119)

Best Pleasure Palaces

Galleria Giorgio Franchetti alla Ca' d'Oro The grandest palace on the Grand Canal, with Venetian Gothic arches. (p124)

Palazzo Ducale Antonio da Ponte's pretty pink Gothic loggia once was the seat of Venetian power. (p44)

Ca' Rezzonico Renaissance grandeur gone baroque. (p78)

Palazzo Grassi Rococo flourishes have been peeled back to reveal neoclassical lines. (p54)

Fondazione Querini Stampalia Baroque beauty with high-modernist updates: Carlo Scarpa-designed gardens and gates, Mario Botta library and cafe. (p141)

Best Modern Marvels

Biennale Pavilions High-modernist pavilion architecture, which showcases radical art and architecture during the Biennales. (p140)

Punta della Dogana Customs warehouses creatively repurposed into cutting-edge installation-art galleries by Tadao Ando. (p78)

Negozio Olivetti Forward-thinking Carlo Scarpa transformed a dusty souvenir shop into a high-tech showcase in 1958. (p57)

Fondazione Giorgio Cini Former naval academy rocks the boat as an avant-garde art gallery. (p157)

Art

Water may be the first thing you notice about Venice, but as you get closer, you'll discover that this city is saturated with art. Canals are just brief interruptions between artworks in this Unesco World Heritage site, with more art treasures than any other city. Through censorship, plague and nonstop parties, Venice kept creating masterpieces.

ANDRIUS GAILIUNAS/SHUTTERSTOCK ©

Best Venetian Masterpieces

Gallerie dell'Accademia Veronese's triumph over censorship: *Feast in the House of Levi*. (p68)

I Frari Titian's red-hot Madonna altarpiece: *Assunta*. (p92)

Scuola Grande di San Rocco Tintoretto to the rescue: *St Mark in Glory*. (p90)

Scuola Dalmata di San Giorgio degli Schiavoni Home to Carpaccio's delightful cycle of paintings of Dalmatian saints George, Tryphone and Jerome. (p140)

Basilica di Santa Maria Assunta Byzantine craftsmen spell out the consequences of dodging biblical commandments in the *Last Judgement*. (p164)

Ca' Pesaro *La Fanciulla del Fiore* by the Venetian Van Gogh, Gino Rossi. (p102)

Best Modern Art Showcases

La Biennale di Venezia The world's most prestigious visual art showcase, held in even-numbered years. (p142)

Peggy Guggenheim Collection Explore the defining collection of breakthrough modern artists. (p72)

Fondazione Giorgio Cini Peter Greenaway videos in Palladio cloisters and blockbuster shows in a naval academy. (p157)

Punta della Dogana Historical customs warehouses retrofitted for hosting installation art exhibitions. (pictured above; p78)

Fondazione Vedova Rotating exhibits powered by robots. (p79)

Casa dei Tre Oci Italian and international exhibitions of contemporary art and photography. (p158)

Fondazione Prada Cutting-edge conceptual art under the gaze of 18th-century frescoes. (p103)

LGBTIQ+

SIMONE PADOVANI/SHUTTERSTOCK ©

Venice's LGBTIQ+ scene is low-key almost to the point of non-existence. There are very few queer-only venues and those that do exist are on the mainland, in and around Mestre. That said, Venice is generally pretty gay-friendly and LGBTIQ+ travellers should feel welcome throughout the city.

Best Events

La Biennale di Venezia A showcase for European art and architecture, La Biennale has provided a platform for LGBTIQ+ themes in recent years. (p142)

Venice International Film Festival The Queer Lion Award is dedicated to films with a homosexual theme. In 2021 it was won by Gianluca Matarrese for his documentary on bondage, *The Last Chapter*.

Best Beaches

Spiaggia degli Alberoni At the southern end of the Lido, this gay-friendly strip was used as a location in Visconti's film *Death in Venice*.

Spiaggia di San Nicolò Another gay-friendly Lido beach, this popular *spiaggia* sits at the far north of the island.

LGBTIQ+ Top Tips

- Gay venues often require membership of Arcigay, Italy's national LGBTIQ+ organisation. Membership cards cost €10 and are available at venues or at **Arcigay Tralaltro** (www.tralaltro.it) in Padua. Padua, an easy 40km from Venice, has an active LGBTIQ+ scene and offers a wider range of gay-friendly night spots than Venice.

- Add Thomas Mann's novella *Death In Venice*, about a writer who becomes obsessed with beautiful young Polish tourist Tadzio, to your Venice reading list. The movie adaptation by Luchino Visconti featured Dirk Bogarde as the ailing artist fixating on the Most Beautiful Boy in the World in a grand hotel on the Lido.

Museums

ALLA IATSUN/SHUTTERSTOCK ©

Peek inside Grand Canal palaces gifted to Venice, and you'll find they're packed with Prada couture, samurai armour and the odd dinosaur. Though he tried, Napoleon couldn't steal all the treasures Venetians had hoarded for centuries. Generous benefactors have restored Venice's treasure-box museums and added plenty to them, too.

Best Venetian Blockbusters

Gallerie dell'Accademia Watch Venetian painters set the world ablaze with saturated colour and censorship-defying art. (p68)

Palazzo Ducale The doge's home decor comprises the world's prettiest propaganda, featuring Veronese, Tintoretto, Tiepolo and Titian. (pictured above; p44)

Museo Correr Palace rooms dedicated to pink Bellinis and blood-red Carpaccios, plus philosophers by Veronese, Titian and Tintoretto in the library. (p54)

Scuola Grande di San Rocco Tintoretto upstages Veronese with action-packed scenes of angelic rescue squads. (p90)

Galleria Giorgio Franchetti alla Ca' d'Oro Baron Franchetti's treasure-box palace packed with masterpieces. (p124)

Best Fashion-Forward Palaces

Museo Fortuny The radical fashion house that freed women from corsets keeps raising eyebrows. (p54)

Fondazione Prada Futurist suits, video art and Duchamp suitcases are making waves along the Grand Canal inside stately Renaissance palace Ca' Corner. (p103)

Palazzo Mocenigo Find fashion inspiration in this palace packed with Venetian glamour. (p102)

Best Modern Art Museums

Peggy Guggenheim Collection Pollock, Rothko, Kandinsky and company make a splash on the Grand Canal. (p72)

Palazzo Grassi Murakami's manic daisies, Damien Hirst's shipwrecked treasures and other provocations in a Grand Canal palace. (p54)

Ca' Pesaro Klimts, Kandinskys and other modern masterpieces Venice slyly snapped up at the Biennale. (p102)

Punta della Dogana Mega-installations are docked inside Venice's ex-customs warehouses. (p78)

Under the Radar

WIRESTOCK CREATORS/SHUTTERSTOCK ©

Best Quiet Neighbourhoods

Castello Escape to this, the quietest of Venice's *sestieri* (districts), to recharge your batteries and mix with the locals in the city's public park.

Cannaregio North of the busy Strada Nova, Cannaregio intrigues with its casual bars and historic Jewish quarter.

Giudecca Across the Giudecca Canal from San Marco, this island is a favourite haunt of artists. Thanks to its lack of major sites, it remains relatively crowd-free.

Torcello The bucolic lagoon island of Torcello, with its sheep and glorious 7th-century basilica, is well worth seeking out.

Best under the Radar Sights

Museo Fortuny A stylish museum hosting creative exhibitions in the salons of art nouveau designer Mariano Fortuny. (pictured above; p54)

Basilica di Santa Maria Assunta Sail out to Torcello to admire glittering mosaics at this 7th-century Byzantine-Romanesque basilica. (p164)

Galleria Giorgio Franchetti alla Ca' d'Oro Artistic treasures dazzle in one of the most beautiful buildings on the Grand Canal. (p124)

Ca' Pesaro Masterpieces of modern art star at this alternative to the vastly more popular Peggy Guggenheim Collection. (p102)

Scala Contarini del Bovolo Escape the San Marco crowds and enjoy rooftop views from atop this 26m-high staircase.

Top Tour Tip

Taking a tour is a great way of discovering Venice's shadows and secret corners. **Best Venice Guides** (http://bestveniceguides.it) has a team of highly qualified guides who can tailor their tours to your specific interests.

For Kids

PABLO DUCROS/SHUTTERSTOCK ©

Adults think Venice is for them, but kids know better. This is where every fairy tale comes to life, where prisoners escape through the roof of a pink palace, Murano glass-blowers breathe life into pocket-sized sea dragons, and ferries and gondolas slide through the waters, beating the school bus hands-down for excitement.

Best Family Attractions

Palazzo Ducale Explore a Gothic prison on the Secret Itineraries tour. (p44)

Torre dell'Orologio Climb this clock tower for giddy views of the bell-chiming figures. (p55)

Museo di Storia Naturale di Venezia Discover dinosaurs and Neanderthal skulls. (p103)

Lido Beaches Sandy beaches and shallow waters make for a perfect escape.

Best Hands-On Learning

Row Venice Hop on and learn to row as gondoliers do. (p130)

Ca' Macana Be inspired and craft your own Carnevale mask. (p84)

Acquolina Cooking School Get to grips with sci-fi-looking lagoon creatures. (p158)

Venice Italian School Order gelato like a pro. (p109)

Best Food

Caffè Florian Hot chocolate in a fairy-tale setting. (pictured above; p41)

Suso Top-notch gelato made from organic ingredients. (p58)

Best Shops

Signor Blum Chunky colourful puzzles, clocks and mobiles, all hand-carved and most featuring Venetian motifs. (p86)

Libreria Marco Polo A great range of kids' books in Italian, perfect for little language learners. (p84)

Apartment Living

Given the expense of eating out, many families opt for staying in an apartment, where they have their own kitchen. Views on Venice (p174) has a good selection of family-friendly apartments.

Island Escapes

Drift away on the blue lagoon, and see where you'll end up next: at a fiery glass-blowing furnace, an organic farmers market at an island prison, or an orphanage that's now a luxury spa. Venice's lagoon offers not only idyllic island retreats – beach clubs, vineyard lunches and farm-stays – but also outlandish escapes from reality.

ALIAKSANDR ANTANOVICH/SHUTTERSTOCK ©

Best Destination Dining

Venissa Osteria Ultra-modern, ocal seafood in an island vineyard. (p170)

Acquastanca Baked goods wedged between glass-blowing studios. (p170)

Trattoria Altanella Authentic Venetian in a vintage trattoria with a flower-hung balcony. (p159)

Locanda Cipriani Wood-beamed dining room, elegant silver service. (p170)

Terra e Acqua Fish risotto aboard a Venetian barge. (p159)

Best Outdoor Attractions

Lido Beaches When temperatures rise, Venice races to the Lido to claim the sandy beachfront.

Museo di Torcello Rare lagoon birds swoop lazily past the Byzantine *campanile* (bell tower) on this wild island. (pictured above; p165)

Venice Kayak Explore the lagoon in peace and quiet under your own steam. (p159)

Vogalonga The regatta is a fine excuse to laze around Mazzorbo, raising toasts to rowers' health. (p170)

Fondazione Giorgio Cini Explore the Borges Labyrinth behind Palladio's cloisters. (p157)

JW Marriott spa Recline poolside at the Marriott's stunning rooftop spa with Venice at your feet. (p161)

Island Tips

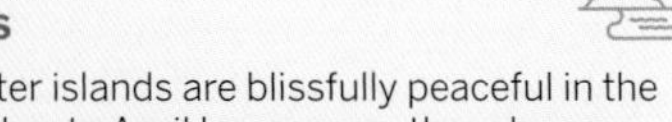

- Outer islands are blissfully peaceful in the October to April low season, though some restaurants and shops close.
- Take binoculars to spot lagoon shorebirds, including white ibises and purple herons.
- Pick up after island picnics to protect Venice's fragile ecosystem.

Responsible Travel

Positive, sustainable and feel-good experiences around the city.

Choose Sustainable Venues

Eat vegan at La Tecia Vegana, and find out that plant-based Italian food is as good as its meat and dairy counterparts. (p81)

Get fishy at restaurants such as Trattoria Altanella, which serves cuttlefish and squid from the nearby waters, and has walls hung with paintings by local artists. (p159)

Give Back

Stay ethically through Fairbnb, which donates to a project chosen by your host: you can visit and perhaps even volunteer with the project. (p174)

Support the city's transformative Made in Prison project by shopping at Process Collettivo, which sells bags and and accessories made from recycled PVC banners. (p112)

Learn More

Learn some Italian at Venice Italian School to go deeper into Venice. (p109)

Take a tour with a local: this provides some employment and enriches your knowledge of this mysterious city – try Best Venice Guides. (p25)

Slow down and learn some of the crafts that Venice is famous for: glass-bead making, mask painting or bookbinding.

Support Local

Shop for local ingredients at the ancient Rialto Market, with all the produce you could ever need to rustle up a delicious *cena* (supper). (p94)

Buy the best in Venice: look out for the Venezia Autentica (https://veneziaautentica.com) label when you are shopping. It is a marker of quality, sustainability and social responsibility.

Leave a Small Footprint

Arrive by train not plane and you will be rewarded with great views along the way – especially if you come via the Alps – and a glorious Grand Canal vision as you exit the station.

CRIS FOTO/SHUTTERSTOCK ©

Take an electric boat from Classic Boats Venice, based on La Certosa. (p159)

Hop onto a traghetto (pictured) to cross the Grand Canal: being sustainably rowed in Venice doesn't need to break the bank. Or take a gondola from a quieter spot away from San Marco, and enjoy an age-old form of eco transport in relative peace.

Resources

Check out We are Here Venice (www.wearehere venice.org), a non-profit organisation dedicated to conserving the city.

To hire a local person for work projects or as a tour guide, check out Venezia Autentica.

Climate Change & Travel

It's impossible to ignore the impact we have when travelling, and the importance of making changes where we can.

Lonely Planet urges all travellers to engage with their travel carbon footprint. There are many carbon calculators online that allow travellers to estimate the carbon emissions generated by their journey; try resurgence.org/resources/carbon-calculator.html. Many airlines and booking sites offer travellers the option of offsetting the impact of greenhouse gas emissions by contributing to climate-friendly initiatives around the world.

We continue to offset the carbon footprint of all Lonely Planet staff travel, while recognising this is a mitigation more than a solution.

Four Perfect Days

Day 1

JAVEN/SHUTTERSTOCK ©

Start with an espresso at **Grancaffè Quadri** (p59) before the Byzantine blitz inside the **Basilica di San Marco** (p40). Browse boutique-lined backstreets to **Museo Fortuny** (p54), the fashion house that created goddess gowns.

Pause at Ponte dell'Accademia for Grand Canal photos, then surrender to the **Gallerie dell' Accademia** (p68). Glimpse gondolas under construction on a waterfront walk along the Zattere. Stop at tiny **Chiesa di San Sebastiano** (p79), packed with Veroneses, then it's '*spritz* o'clock' in lively **Campo Santa Margherita** (pictured; p174).

Leap back into the 1700s at nearby **Scuola Grande dei Carmini** (p79), the evocative setting for costumed classical concerts.

Day 2

ALEKSANDR MEDVEDKOV/SHUTTERSTOCK ©

Kick off day two spotting lagoon delicacies at **Rialto Market** (p94), side-stepping to **Drogheria Mascari** (p97) for gourmet goods. Head to Gothic show-off **I Frari** (p92) and its sunny Titian altarpiece. Then slip into **Scuola Grande di San Rocco** (p90) for prime-time-drama Tintorettos.

Explore modern art at the **Peggy Guggenheim Collection** (p72), and contrast it with contemporary **Punta della Dogana** (p78). Duck into domed **Basilica di Santa Maria della Salute** (pictured; p78) for Titians and legendary curative powers, then cross the Grand Canal on Venice's only wooden bridge, **Ponte dell'Accademia**.

Hear an opera at **La Fenice** (p63), or experience Vivaldi by **Interpreti Veneziani** (p49).

Day 3

VIOLETA MELETI/SHUTTERSTOCK ©

Stroll Riva degli Schiavoni for views across the lagoon to Palladio's **Basilica di San Giorgio Maggiore** (p152), then seek out Castello's hidden wonder: **Chiesa di San Francesco della Vigna** (p140).

Dip into pretty **Chiesa di Santa Maria dei Miracoli** (pictured; p124) – a marble miracle made from the Basilica di San Marco's leftovers – before wandering serene *fondamente* (canal banks) past Moorish statues ringing Campo dei Mori to reach **Chiesa della Madonna dell'Orto** (p124). Then tour the **Ghetto's synagogues** (p118) until Venice's happiest hours beckon across the bridge at **Al Timon** (p121).

Finally, take a romantic gondola ride through Cannaregio's long canals.

Day 4

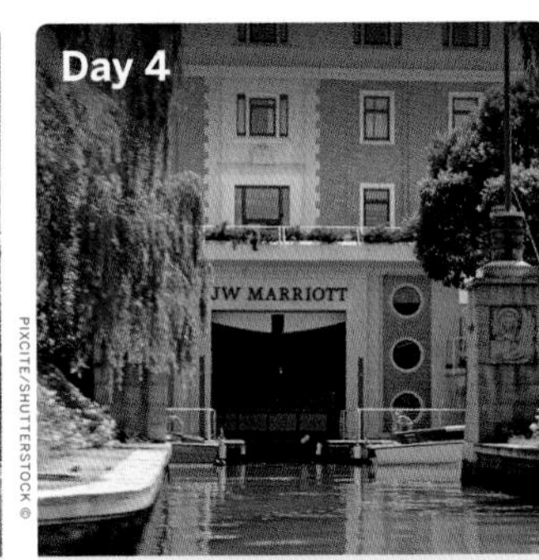

PIXCITE/SHUTTERSTOCK ©

Take a *vaporetto* (small passenger ferry) for Torcello and Burano. Follow the sheep trail to Torcello's Byzantine **Basilica di Santa Maria Assunta** (p164), where the apse's golden Madonna calmly stares down. Catch the boat back to Burano to admire handmade lace at **Museo del Merletto** (p169).

Take in the fiery passions of glass artisans at Murano's legendary *fornaci* (furnaces), and see glass showcased at **Museo del Vetro** (p167). Hop the *vaporetto* to Giudecca to relax at the **JW Marriott spa** (pictured; p161), with views of San Marco across glassy waters.

Celebrate your tour of the lagoon with a prosecco toast and tango across Piazza San Marco at time-warped **Caffè Florian** (p41); repeat as necessary.

Need to Know

For detailed information, see Survival Guide (p173)

Currency
euro (€)

Language
Italian, Venetian dialect

Visas
Not required for EU citizens. Nationals of the UK, Australia, Brazil, Canada, Japan, New Zealand and the USA do not need visas for visits of up to 90 days.

Money
You can pay by card almost everywhere, but keep some cash handy.

Mobile Phones
GSM and tri-band phones can be used with a local SIM card.

Time
GMT/UTC plus one hour during winter; GMT/UTC plus two hours during summer daylight saving.

Tipping
Optional 10% at restaurants; at least €2 per bag or night, for porter, maid or room service.

Daily Budget

Budget: Less than €120
Dorm bed: €35–60

Cicheti (bar snacks) at All'Arco: €5–15

Spritz (prosecco cocktail): €2.50–4

Midrange: €120–250
B&B: €70–180

Civic Museum Pass: €40

Midrange dinner: €35–40

Top End: More than €250
Boutique hotel: from €200

Gondola ride: €80

Top-end dinner: from €50

Advance Planning

Two months before Book high-season accommodation and tickets to La Fenice, Venice Film Festival premieres and Biennale openings.

Three weeks before Check special-event calendars at www.veneziadavivere.com.

One week before Make restaurant reservations for a big night out; skip the queues by booking tickets to major attractions, exhibitions and events online at www.veneziaunica.it.

Arriving in Venice

Most people arrive in Venice by train or plane. There is a long-distance bus service to the city and it is also possible to drive to Venice.

Stazione Venezia Santa Lucia

Regional and international trains run frequently to Venice's Santa Lucia train station (www.veneziasantalucia.it), appearing on signs as 'Ferrovia' within Venice. You can obtain a map and buy *vaporetto* (small ferry) tickets from the tourist office opposite platform 3. *Vaporetti* connect the station with all parts of Venice.

Marco Polo Airport

Marco Polo Airport (www.veniceairport.it) is Venice's main international airport and is located in Tessera, 12km east of Mestre. The terminal has ticket offices for water taxis and Alilaguna water bus transfers.

Getting Around

Walking is the most scenic and easiest way to get around Venice. The other way to navigate this city on the water is by boat. Cars and bicycles can be used on the Lido.

Vaporetto

These small passenger ferries are Venice's main public transport – note the line and direction of travel at the dock.

Gondola

Not mere transport but an adventure – and the best way to slip into Venice's smaller canals.

Water Taxi

The only door-to-door option, but fares are steep.

Traghetto

Daytime cash-only public gondola service (€2) to cross the Grand Canal between bridges.

Venice Neighbourhoods

Campo del Ghetto Nuovo & the Ghetto

Rialto Market

Scuola Grande di San Rocco

I Frari

Peggy Guggenhe… Collectio…

Gallerie dell' Accademia

San Polo & Santa Croce (p89)
Shop for fresh market produce, rub shoulders with divine art and indulge in some of Venice's best culinary adventures.

Dorsoduro & the Accademia (p67)
Explore fine art and golden-age splendour, all with prime Grand Canal waterfront views and a dash of nightlife.

San Marco & Palazzo Ducale (p39)
Packed with attractions (and people), from the basilica to the Ducal Palace, this is unmissable Venice.

Murano, Burano & the Northern Islands (p163)
Head north across the shimmering waters to Murano's glass heaven, rainbow-hued Burano, the legendary isle of Torcello, and more.

Cannaregio & the Ghetto (p117)
Graze on *cicheti* (Venetian tapas) at neighbourhood bars, get lost in beguiling backstreets and explore the evocative Jewish quarter.

Castello (p135)
Venice's largest 'hood faces the lagoon, with palaces, the Arsenale and the city's gardens, home to the Biennale.

Basilica di San Marco

Palazzo Ducale

Basilica di San Giorgio Maggiore

Giudecca, Lido & the Southern Islands (p151)
A hop south on the lagoon are culture and crafts on tranquil Giudecca, and laidback beach life (and cars!) on the Lido.

Explore Venice

Venice's Walking & Cycling Tours

Venice rooftops INGUS KRUKLITIS/SHUTTERSTOCK ©

Explore San Marco & Palazzo Ducale

There are so many world-class attractions in San Marco that some visitors never leave – while others are reluctant to visit, fearing crowds. But why miss the pleasures of the Basilica di San Marco, Palazzo Ducale, Museo Correr and jewel-box La Fenice? But don't stop there. The backstreets are packed with galleries, restaurants, boutiques and bars.

The Short List

- ***Basilica di San Marco (p40)*** *Joining the chorus of gasps at Venice's showpiece cathedral.*
- ***Palazzo Ducale (p44)*** *Marvelling at the lavish state rooms and dingy prisons at this Gothic landmark.*
- ***Teatro La Fenice (p63)*** *Bellowing 'Bravo/a!' for an encore at Venice's jewel-box opera house.*
- ***Museo Correr (p54)*** *Coming face to face with philosophers painted by Veronese and Tintoretto.*
- ***Caffè Florian (p49)*** *Sipping sunset drinks at Venice's most revered cafe.*

Getting There & Around

Vaporetto Line 1 serves stops on the Grand Canal; line 2 is faster and stops at Rialto, San Samuele and San Marco Giardinetti.

Traghetto A gondola ferry crosses the Grand Canal from Santa Maria del Giglio.

Follow yellow-signed shortcuts from Rialto through shop-lined Marzarie to Piazza San Marco. It's often quicker than the *vaporetto*.

San Marco & Palazzo Ducale Map on p52

Campanile (p55) and Palazzo Ducale (p44)

Top Experience

Marvel at Dome Mosaics at Basilica di San Marco

MAP P52, G4

St Mark's Basilica

www.basilicasanmarco.it

In a city packed with architectural wonders, nothing beats Basilica di San Marco for sheer spectacle and bombastic exuberance. In AD 828, wily Venetian merchants allegedly smuggled St Mark's corpse out of Egypt in a barrel of pork fat to avoid inspection by Muslim authorities. Venice built a basilica around its stolen saint in keeping with the city's own sense of supreme self-importance.

Construction

Church authorities in Rome took a dim view of Venice's tendency to glorify itself and God in the same breath, but the city defiantly created a private chapel for their doge that outshone Venice's official cathedral (St Peter's Basilica in Castello) in every conceivable way. After the original Basilica di San Marco was burned down during an uprising, Venice rebuilt the basilica two more times (mislaying and rediscovering the saint's body along the way). The current incarnation was completed in 1094, reflecting the city's cosmopolitan image, with Byzantine domes, a Greek cross layout and walls clad in marbles looted from Syria, Egypt and Palestine.

Facade

The front of the basilica ripples and crests like a wave, its five niched portals capped with shimmering mosaics and frothy stonework arches, with four bronze horses waving their hooves above the central doorway. It is especially resplendent just before sunset, when the sun's dying rays set the golden mosaics ablaze. Grand entrances are made through the central portal, under an ornate triple arch featuring Egyptian purple porphyry columns and intricate 13th- to 14th-century stone reliefs. The oldest mosaic on the facade, dating from 1270, is in the lunette above the far-left portal, depicting St Mark's stolen body arriving at the basilica. The theme is echoed in three of the other lunettes, including the 1660 mosaics above the second portal from the right, showing turbaned officials recoiling from the hamper of pork fat containing the saintly corpse.

Dome Mosaics

Blinking is natural upon your first glimpse of the basilica's 8500 sq metres of glittering mosaics, many made with 24-carat gold leaf fused onto the back of the glass to represent divine light.

★ Top Tips

- Dress modestly (ie knees and shoulders covered) and leave large bags at the **Ateneo San Basso Left Luggage Office**.
- Reserve a ticket in advance through the website and head directly into the central portal. Present your voucher at the entrance.
- Otherwise, the best chance of beating the crowds is to get here 30 minutes before opening time and wait for the doors to open.
- The extra fee for the museum is well worth it, giving you a bird's-eye view of the interior and the bronze horses, as well as sweeping Venice vistas.

Take a Break

Bask in the afterglow of the basilica's golden magnificence in the jewellery-box interior of Caffè Florian (p49).

Just inside the narthex (vestibule) glitter the basilica's oldest mosaics, **Apostles with the Madonna**, standing sentry by the main door for more than 950 years. The atrium's medieval **Dome of Genesis** depicts the separation of sky and water with surprisingly abstract motifs, anticipating modern art by 650 years.

Inside the church proper, three golden domes vie for your attention. The images are intended to be read from the altar end to the entry, so the **Cupola of the Prophets** shimmers above the main altar, while the **Last Judgement** is depicted in the vault above the entrance (and best seen from the museum). The dome nearest the door is the **Pentecost Cupola**, showing the Holy Spirit represented by a dove shooting tongues of flame onto the heads of the surrounding saints. In the central 13th-century **Ascension Cupola**, angels swirl around the central figure of Christ hovering among the stars. Scenes from St Mark's life unfold around the main altar, which houses the saint's simple stone **sarcophagus**.

Pala d'Oro

Tucked behind the main **altar**, this stupendous golden screen is studded with 2000 emeralds, amethysts, sapphires, rubies, pearls and other gemstones. But the most priceless treasures here are biblical figures in vibrant cloisonné, begun in Constantinople in 976 CE and elaborated by Venetian goldsmiths in 1209. Four apostles surround Jesus writing their gospels with their eyes fixed on him, as he glances sideways at a

Basilica di San Marco exterior

studious St Mark. Mary, immediately below Jesus, throws up her hands in wonder – an understandable reaction to such a captivating scene.

Treasury

Holy bones and booty from the Crusades fill the **Tesoro**, including a 4th-century rock-crystal lamp, a 10th-century rock-crystal ewer with winged feet made for Fatimid Caliph al-'Aziz-bi-llah, and an exquisite enamelled 10th-century Byzantine chalice. Don't miss the bejewelled 12th-century Archangel Michael icon, featuring tiny, feisty enamelled saints that look ready to break free of their golden setting and mount a miniature attack on evil. In a separate room, velvet-padded boxes preserve the remains of sainted doges alongside the usual assortment of credulity-challenging relics: St Roch's femur, the arm St George used to slay the dragon and even a lock of the Madonna's hair.

Museum

Accessed by a narrow staircase leading up from the basilica's atrium, the **Museo di San Marco** transports visitors to the level of the church's rear mosaics and out onto the **Loggia dei Cavalli**, the terrace above the main facade. The four magnificent bronze horses positioned here are actually reproductions of the precious 2nd-century originals, plundered from Constantinople's hippodrome, displayed inside.

Architecture buffs will revel in the beautifully rendered drawings and scale models of the basilica. In the displays of 13th- to 16th-century mosaic fragments, the Prophet Abraham is all ears and raised eyebrows, as though scandalised by Venetian gossip. A corridor leads into a section of the Palazzo Ducale containing the **doge's banquet hall**, where dignitaries wined and dined among lithe stucco figures of *Music*, *Poetry* and *Peace*.

Top Experience

Indulge in History at Palazzo Ducale

Don't be fooled by its genteel Gothic elegance: behind that lacy pink-and-white patterned facade, the doge's palace shows serious muscle and a steely will to survive. The seat of Venice's government for more than seven centuries, this powerhouse stood the test of storms, crashes and conspiracies – only to be outwitted by Casanova, the notorious seducer who escaped from the attic prison.

MAP P52, H5

Ducal Palace

www.palazzoducale.visitmuve.it

Architecture

After fire gutted the original palace in 1577, Antonio da Ponte restored its Gothic grandeur. The white Istrian stone and Veronese pink marble palace caps a graceful colonnade with medieval capitals depicting key Venetian guilds. The pretty arcaded **loggia** along the *piazzetta* (little square) served a solemn purpose: death sentences were read between the ninth and 10th columns from the left.

Courtyard

Entering through the colonnaded courtyard (pictured), you'll spot Sansovino's brawny statues of Apollo and Neptune flanking Antonio Rizzo's **Scala dei Giganti** (Giants' Staircase). Just off the courtyard in the wing facing the square is the **Museo dell'Opera**, displaying a collection of stone columns and capitals from previous incarnations of the building.

Doge's Apartments

The doge's suite of private rooms takes up a large chunk of the 1st floor above the loggia. This space is now used for temporary art exhibitions, which are ticketed separately (around €10 extra). The doge lived like a prisoner in his gilded suite in the palace, which he could not leave without permission. Still, consider the real estate: a terrace garden with private entry to the basilica, and a dozen salons with splendidly restored marble fireplaces carved by Tullio and Antonio Lombardo. The most intriguing room is the **Sala dello Scudo** (Shield Room), covered with world maps that reveal the extent of Venetian power (and the limits of its cartographers) c 1483 and 1762.

Sala delle Quattro Porte

From the loggia level, head to the top of Sansovino's 24-carat gilt stuccowork **Scala d'Oro**

★ Top Tips

- Book tickets online in advance to avoid queues.
- Tickets (valid for three months) include Museo Correr (p54) but it's worth paying extra for a Museum Pass, which gives access to several other high-profile civic museums.
- Last admission is one hour prior to closing.
- Don't leave your trip until too late in the day, as some parts of the palace, such as the prisons, may close early.
- Get here when the doors open to avoid groups, which start arriving at around 9.30am to 10am.

Take a Break

Call into the earthy but excellent **Pasticceria da Bonifacio** for a counter-top coffee, pastry or *spritz*.

(Golden Staircase) and emerge into rooms covered with gorgeous propaganda. In Palladio-designed **Sala delle Quattro Porte** (Hall of the Four Doors), ambassadors awaited ducal audiences under a lavish display of Venice's virtues by Giovanni Cambi. Other convincing shows of Venetian superiority include Titian's 1576 *Doge Antonio Grimani Kneeling Before Faith* amid approving cherubs and Tiepolo's 1740s *Venice Receiving Gifts of the Sea from Neptune*, where Venice is a gorgeous blonde casually leaning on a lion.

Anticollegio

Delegations waited in the **Anticollegio** (Council Antechamber), where Tintoretto drew parallels between Roman gods and Venetian government: *Mercury and the Three Graces* reward Venice's industriousness with beauty, and *Minerva Dismissing Mars* is a Venetian triumph of savvy over brute force. The recently restored ceiling is Veronese's 1577 *Venice Distributing Honours*, while on the walls is a vivid reminder of diplomatic behaviour to avoid: Veronese's *Rape of Europe*.

Collegio & Sala del Senato

Few were granted an audience in the Palladio-designed **Collegio** (Council Chamber), where Veronese's 1575–78 *Virtues of the Republic* ceiling shows Venice as a bewitching blonde waving her sceptre like a wand over Justice and Peace. Father–son team Jacopo and Domenico Tintoretto attempt similar flattery, showing Venice keeping

Ceiling of the Sala Consiglio dei Dieci

company with Apollo, Mars and Mercury in their *Triumph of Venice* ceiling for the **Sala del Senato** (Senate Chamber).

Sala Consiglio dei Dieci

Government cover-ups were never so appealing as in the **Sala Consiglio dei Dieci** (Chamber of the Council of Ten), where Venice's star chamber plotted under Veronese's *Juno Bestowing her Gifts on Venice*, a glowing goddess strewing gold ducats. Over the slot where anonymous treason accusations were slipped into the **Sala della Bussola** (Compass Room) is the *St Mark in Glory* ceiling.

Sala del Maggior Consiglio

The grandest room on the 1st floor is the cavernous 1419 **Sala del Maggior Consiglio** (Grand Council Chamber). The doge's throne once stood in front of the staggering 22m-by-7m *Paradise* backdrop (by Domenico Tintoretto) where heaven is crammed with 500 prominent Venetians, including several Tintoretto patrons. Veronese's political posturing is more elegant in his oval *Apotheosis of Venice* ceiling, where gods marvel at Venice's coronation by angels.

Secret Itineraries Tours

Further rooms can be visited on the fascinating 75-minute **Secret Itineraries tour**. It takes in the cells known as **pozzi** (wells) and the unadorned **Council of Ten Secret Headquarters**. Beyond this ominous office suite, the **Chancellery** is lined with drawers of top-secret files, including reports by Venice's far-reaching spy network. The accused might be led to the windowless **torture Chamber**. Upstairs lie the **piombi** (Leads), the attic prison where Casanova was held in 1756. As described in his memoirs, he made an ingenious escape through the roof. He would later return to Venice, enlisted as a spy for the Council of Ten.

Walking Tour

Music in San Marco

Once Venice's dominion over the high seas ended, it discovered the power of high Cs, hiring as San Marco choirmaster Claudio Monteverdi, the father of modern opera, and bringing on baroque with Antonio Vivaldi. Today, music apps still can't compare with Venice's live-music offerings. While Teatro La Fenice is the obvious draw for opera lovers, try these other music destinations to immerse yourself in a Venetian soundtrack.

Walk Facts

Start Caffè Lavena; *vaporetto* San Marco

Finish Chiesa San Vidal; *vaporetto* Accademia

Length 1.5km; ¾ hour

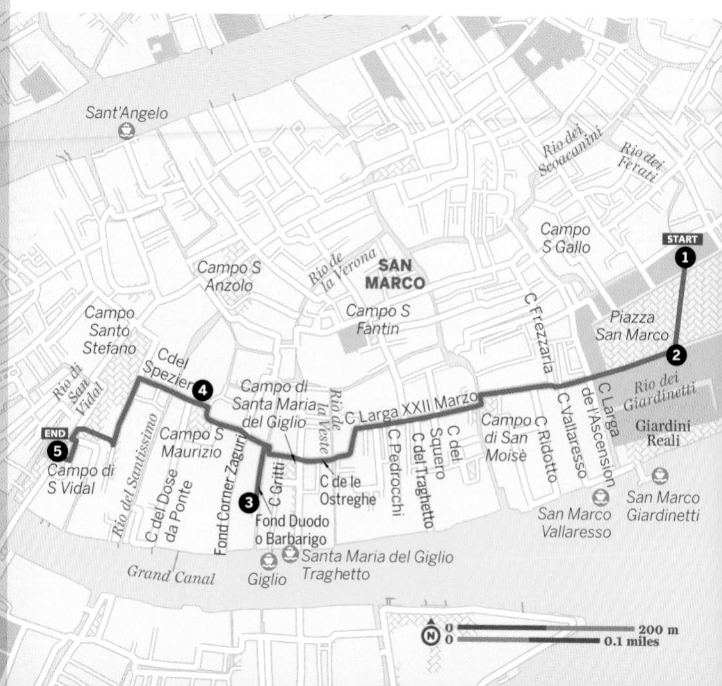

❶ Caffè Lavena

Opera composer Richard Wagner had the right idea: when Venice leaves you weak in the knees, get a pick-me-up at **Lavena**. An espresso at Lavena's mirrored bar is a baroque bargain, though you may be put off by the Murano glass 'Moor's head' chandeliers. Spring for piazza seating to savour *caffè corretto* (coffee 'corrected' with liquor) accompanied by Lavena's nimble violinists.

❷ Caffè Florian

Caffè Florian (www.caffeflorian.com) maintains rituals established around 1720: white-jacketed waiters serve cappuccino on silver trays, and the orchestra strikes up as sunset illuminates San Marco's mosaics. Piazza seating during concerts costs €6 extra, but dreamy-eyed romantics in the footsteps of Madame de Staël, Byron and Dickens hardly notice. Among Italy's first bars to welcome women and revolutionaries, Florian's radical-chic reputation persists with its art exhibits.

❸ Musica a Palazzo

Hang onto your prosecco: it's always high drama in the historic salons of **Musica a Palazzo**. The beautiful Venetian baroque palace overlooking the Grand Canal provides a unique, intimate setting as the audience follows the action from hall to hall, surrounded by authentic artworks and furnishings.

❹ Museo della Musica

Housed in the restored neoclassical Chiesa di San Maurizio, **Museo della Musica** presents a collection of rare 17th- to 20th-century instruments, accompanied by informative panels on the life and times of Venice's Antonio Vivaldi. The museum is funded by Interpreti Veneziani.

❺ Bravado at Interpreti Veneziani

Everything you've heard of Vivaldi from weddings and mobile ringtones is proved fantastically wrong by **Interpreti Veneziani** (www.interpretiveneziani.com), who play Vivaldi on 18th-century instruments at **Chiesa San Vidal** as a soundtrack for living in this city of intrigue – you'll never listen to *The Four Seasons* again without hearing summer storms erupting over the lagoon, or snow-muffled footsteps hurrying over footbridges on a winter's night.

Walking Tour

San Marco Royal Tour

Dukes and dignitaries had the run of San Marco for centuries, and now it's your turn, on this royal tour that ends with your own palace intrigue.

Walk Facts

Start Giardini Reali; *vaporetto* San Marco

Finish Scala Contarini del Bovolo; *vaporetto* Sant'Angelo

Length 3km; 1½ hours

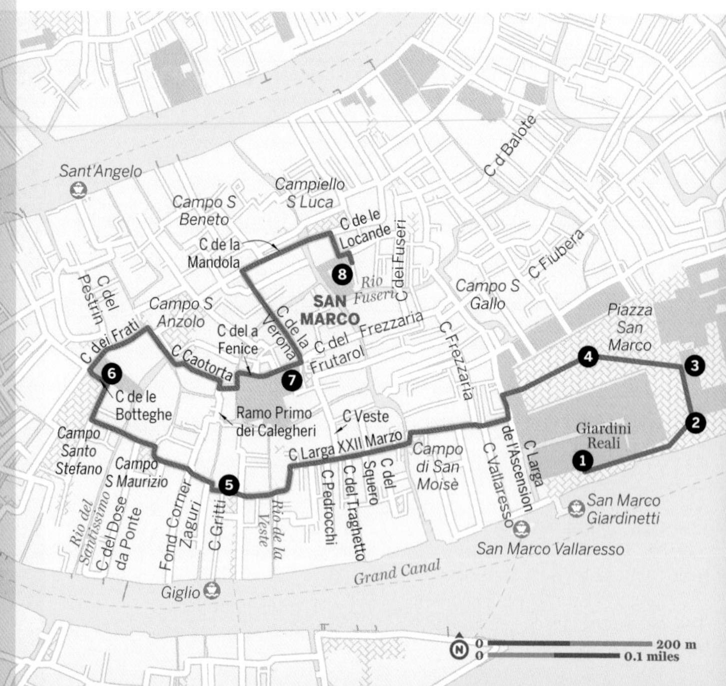

❶ Giardini Reali

In a city low on greenery, start with a stroll under the wisteria-wrapped pergola of the tranquil **royal gardens**, established under Napoleon's rule and remodelled in 2019.

❷ Columns of San Marco

Venetians still hurry past these **granite pillars**, site of public executions for centuries.

❸ Palazzo Ducale

Pass by the **Ducal Palace** loggia, where doges once lived in gilded imprisonment, and punishments were publicly announced before they were posted on the palace door.

❹ Piazza San Marco

In **Piazza San Marco**, turn your back on the **Basilica di San Marco** (p40) to face Ala Napoleonica. Napoleon brazenly razed San Geminiano church to build this palace, which today houses the entry to the **Museo Correr** (p54). The right-hand arcade flanking the piazza is Mauro Codussi's 16th-century **Procuratie Vecchie**.

❺ Chiesa di Santa Maria del Giglio

Take Calle Larga XXII Marzo towards this baroque **church** (p56), whose exterior is sculpted with maps of Rome and five cities that were Venetian possessions at the time.

❻ Chiesa di Santo Stefano

Stop to admire Bartolomeo Bon's marble Gothic portals as you walk past **St Steven's Church** (p54), and then continue around to the Campo Sant'Anzolo and look back. The church's free-standing bell tower leans 2m, as though it's had one *spritz* too many.

❼ Teatro La Fenice

After pausing to take note of Venice's much rebuilt opera house, **La Fenice** (p63), take canyon-like Calle de la Verona into the shadows and continue on to Calle dei Assassini. Corpses were so frequently found here that in 1128, Venice banned the full beards assassins wore as disguises.

❽ Scala Contarini del Bovolo

Kissing in *campi* (squares) is such an established Venetian pastime it's surprising doges didn't tax it – duck into Renaissance **Scala Contarini del Bovolo** (p57) courtyard for privacy.

Take a Break

Engaging staff serve up tasty *cicheti* (Venetian tapas) from a central horseshoe-shaped bar in gleaming, compact Black-Jack (p61).

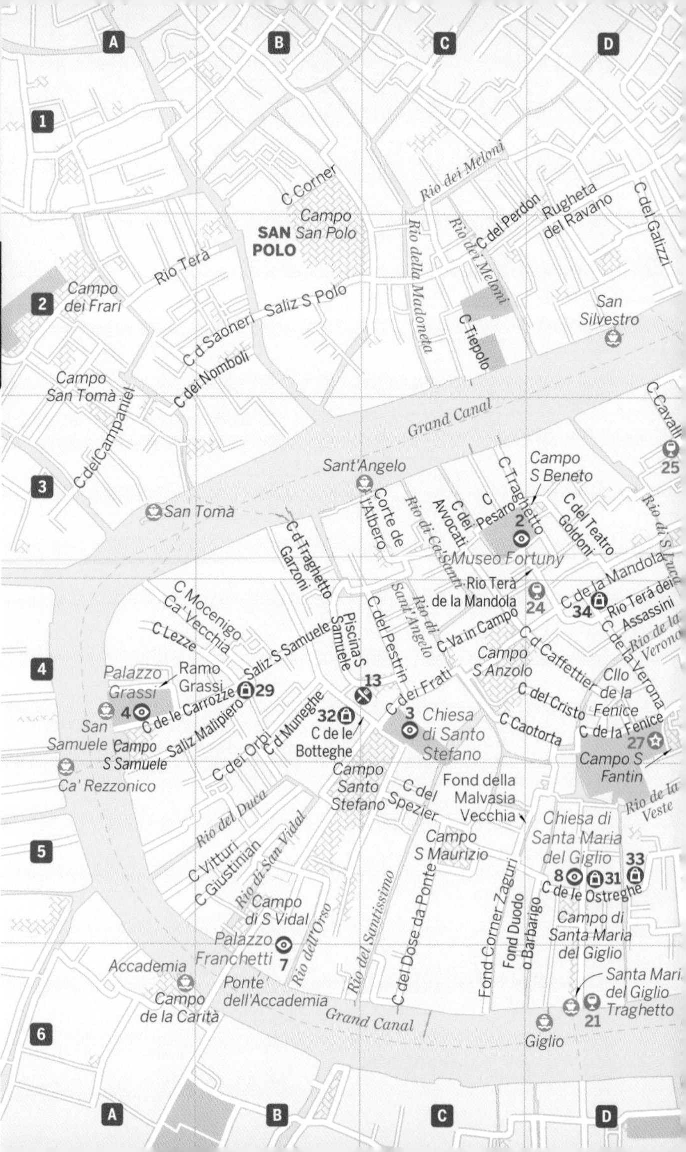

A B C D

1

2

3

4

5

6

C Corner
Campo San Polo
SAN POLO
Rio dei Meloni
Rio della Madoneta
Rio dei Meloni
C del Perdon
Rugheta del Ravano
C del Galizzi
Rio Terà
Campo dei Frari
Saliz S Polo
C d Saoneri
C dei Nomboli
C Tiepolo
San Silvestro
Campo San Tomà
C del Campaniel
Grand Canal
C Cavalli
25
Sant'Angelo
Campo S Beneto
C Traghetto
C Pesaro
C dei Avvocati
Rio di Ca' Santi
Corte de l'Albero
C del Teatro Goldoni
Rio di S Luca
San Tomà
C d Traghetto Garzoni
2
Museo Fortuny
Rio Terà de la Mandola
24
C de la Mandola
34
Rio Terà dei Assassini
Rio de la Verona
C Mocenigo Ca' Vecchia
C Lezze
Piscina S Samuele
C del Pestrin
Rio di Sant'Angelo
C Va in Campo
Campo S Anzolo
C d Caffettier
C de la Verona
Saliz S Samuele
Palazzo Grassi
Ramo Grassi
29
13
C dei Frati
Cllo de la Fenice
C del Cristo
4
C de le Carrozze
San Samuele
Saliz Malipiero
C d Muneghe
32
C de le Botteghe
3
Chiesa di Santo Stefano
C Caotorta
C de la Fenice
27
Campo S Samuele
C dei Orbi
Campo S Fantin
Ca' Rezzonico
Campo Santo Stefano
C del Spezier
Fond della Malvasia Vecchia
Rio del Duca
Chiesa di Santa Maria del Giglio
Rio de la Veste
Campo S Maurizio
33
C Vitturi
C Giustinian
Rio di San Vidal
8
31
C de le Ostreghe
Campo di S Vidal
Rio del Santissimo
C del Dose da Ponte
Fond Corner Zaguri
Fond Duodo o Barbarigo
Campo di Santa Maria del Giglio
Palazzo Franchetti
7
Rio dell'Orso
Accademia
Santa Mari del Giglio Traghetto
Ponte dell'Accademia
Campo de la Carità
Grand Canal
21
Giglio

A B C D

E F G H

0 200 m
0 0.1 miles

1

Ponte di Rialto

Saliz del Fontego dei Tedeschi

RIALTO

C del Sturion

Saliz Pio X

Campo San Bartolomeo

14

Riva del Vin

Rialto

C d Bombaseri

19

C Ponte S Antonio

C Carminati

C d Fava

Saliz San Lio

Fond dei Preti

Rio di S Maria Formosa

Campo Santa Maria Formosa

2

C Larga Mazzini

Via 2 Aprile

C Galeazza

C dei Stagneri

CASTELLO

C d Paradiso

Riva del Carbon

C Bembo

Campo della Fava

Marzaria

Campo San Salvador

C de la Malvasia

C S Antonio

C de la Guerra

Corte del Teatro

28

C del Lovo

C d Balote

35

C de le Acque

C del Carbon

C Loredan

C dei Fabbri

Rio di San Salvador

Campo della Guerra

Rio del Vin

16

Campo San Luca

Marzaria S Zulian

C dei Specchieri

C d Rimedio

Campo Manin

26

C d Gambaro

Rio Terà Paternian

12

Rio dei Scoacanini

Rio dei Ferali

3

C Goldoni

C d Preti

18

Marzaria de l'Orologio

Rio di Palazzo della Paglia

15

C de le Locande

C dei Fuseri

C d Schiavine

C Fiubera

C Larga San Marco

Rio Fuseri

Rio Terà de le Colonne

9

30

Corte Zorzi

Scala Contarini del Bovolo

Campo S Gallo

Rio del Procurate

C d Selvadego

5

Pasticceria da Bonifacio

11

Torre dell'Orologio

Basilica di San Marco

C dei Albanesi

Frezzaria

Rio Orseolo

20

4

C del Lutarol

SAN MARCO

C Zorzi

Bacino Orseolo

Negozio Olivetti

Campanile

Rio dei Barcaroli

C Frezzaria

10

6

C d la Chiesa

C del Carro

C Bognolo

Piazza San Marco

1

17

Museo Correr

Palazzo Ducale

Ramo 1 Corte Contarina

San Zaccaria

C Veste

Rio dei Giardinetti

C Larga XXII Marzo

C Vallaresso

Giardini Reali

5

C del Squero

C del Traghetto

C Ridotto

C dei 13 Martiri

San Marco Giardinetti

22

Corte Barozzi

23

C Pedrocchi

Alilaguna Fast Ferry to Airport

San Marco Vallaresso

Fond del Fontegheto

Bacino di San Marco

6

E F G H

For reviews see

Top Experiences	p40
Sights	p54
Eating	p57
Drinking	p59
Entertainment	p63
Shopping	p64

Sights

Museo Correr MUSEUM

1 MAP P52, F4

Napoleon pulled down an ancient church to build his royal digs over Piazza San Marco, and then filled them with the riches of the doges while taking some of Venice's finest heirlooms to France as trophies. When he lost Venice to the Austrians, Empress Sissi remodelled the palace, adding ceiling frescoes, silk cladding and brocade curtains. It's now open to the public and full of many of Venice's reclaimed treasures, including ancient maps, statues including Antonio Canova's 1776 star-crossed lovers Orpheus and Eurydice, cameos and canvases. (www.correr.visitmuve.it)

Museo Fortuny MUSEUM

2 MAP P52, C3

Find design inspiration at the palatial home studio of art nouveau designer Mariano Fortuny y Madrazo (1871–1949), whose uncorseted Delphi-goddess frocks set the standard for bohemian chic. The 1st-floor salon walls are eclectic mood boards: Fortuny fashions and Isfahan tapestries, family portraits, artfully peeling plaster and the maestro's famous silk and glass lamps. Intriguing temporary exhibitions spread from the basement to the attic, the best of which use the general ambience of grand decay to great effect. (www.fortuny.visitmuve.it)

Chiesa di Santo Stefano CHURCH

3 MAP P52, C4

The free-standing bell tower, visible from the square behind, leans disconcertingly, but this brick Gothic church has stood tall since the 13th century. Credit for shipshape splendour goes to Bartolomeo Bon for the marble entry portal and to Venetian shipbuilders, who constructed the vast wooden *carena di nave* (ship's keel) ceiling that resembles an upturned Noah's ark. (www.chorusvenezia.org)

Palazzo Grassi GALLERY

4 MAP P52, A4

Grand Canal gondola riders gaze at the massive sculptures by contemporary artists docked in front of Giorgio Masari's neoclassical palace (built 1748–72). The provocative art collection of French billionaire François Pinault overflows Palazzo Grassi, while clever curation and art-star name-dropping are the hallmarks of rotating temporary exhibits. Despite all this artistic glamour, it's Tadao Ando's interior architecture that steals the show, with origami folds of gleaming white concrete. (www.palazzograssi.it)

Torre dell'Orologio LANDMARK

5 MAP P52, G4

The two hardest-working men in Venice stand duty on a rooftop around the clock, one old and one young to show the passing of time. The 'Do Mori' (Two Moors) exposed to the elements atop the Torre dell'Orologio (clock tower) are made of bronze, and their bell-hammering mechanism runs like, well, clockwork. Below the Moors (though some think the statues were intended to depict shepherds), Venice's gold-leafed 15th-century timepiece tracks lunar phases. Visits are by guided tour; bookings are essential. (https://torreorologio.visitmuve.it/)

Campanile TOWER

6 MAP P52, G4

Basilica di San Marco's 99m-tall bell tower has been rebuilt twice since its initial construction in 888 CE, most recently in 1912, following a dramatic collapse 10 years earlier. Galileo Galilei tested his telescope here in 1609 but modern-day visitors head to the top for 360-degree lagoon views and close encounters with the **Marangona**, the booming bronze bell that originally signalled the start and end of the working day for the *marangoni* (artisans) at the Arsenale shipyards. Today it rings twice a day, at noon and midnight. (www.basilicasanmarco.it)

Torre dell'Orologio (left) and Basilica di San Marco (right; p40)

Palazzo Franchetti PALACE

7 MAP P52, B6

This 16th-century *palazzo* (mansion) passed through the hands of various Venetian families before Archduke Frederik of Austria snapped it up and set about modernising it. The Comte de Chambord (aka King Henry V of France in exile) continued the work, while the Franchetti family, who lived here after independence, restored its Gothic fairy-tale look and introduced a fantastical art nouveau staircase dripping with dragons. It's now used for art exhibitions, although the works have to compete with showstopping Murano chandeliers. (www.palazzofranchetti.it)

Chiesa di Santa Maria del Giglio CHURCH

8 MAP P52, D5

Founded in the 9th century but almost completely rebuilt in the late 17th century, this church is distinguished by a series of six relief maps on its facade featuring Rome and five cities that were Venetian possessions at the time: Padua, the Croatian cities of Zadar and Split, and the Greek cities of Heraklion and Corfu. Inside are some intriguing masterpieces, including Ruben's sweetly voluptuous *Madonna with Baby and San Giovannino*. (www.chorusvenezia.org)

Water taxi outside Palazzo Franchetti

Scala Contarini del Bovolo

NOTABLE BUILDING

Under the Republic, only the Church and state were permitted to erect towers, as the structures could conceivably be used for military purposes. In around 1400 the Contarini family, eager to show off their wealth and power, cheekily built this non-tower instead. Combining Venetian Gothic, Byzantine and Renaissance elements, this romantic 'staircase' looks even higher than its 26m due to the simple trick of decreasing the height of the arches as it rises. (www.gioiellinascostidivenezia.com)

Negozio Olivetti

ARCHITECTURE

10 MAP P52, F4

Ultramodern Negozio Olivetti was an outright provocation when it first appeared under the frilly arcades of the Procuratie Vecchie in 1958. High-tech pioneer Olivetti commissioned Venetian architect Carlo Scarpa to transform a narrow, dim souvenir shop into a showcase for its sleek typewriters and 'computing machines' (several 1948–54 models are displayed). (www.negoziolivetti.it)

See Venice Like a Venetian

Throughout San Marco you'll be tripping over smart-phone-touting tourists. Everyone, it seems, wants to capture the perfect Venetian scene. Getty photojournalist and Venetian Marco Secchi will show you how during an in-depth **photo tour** (www.venicephototour.com) exploring the secret corners of the city. In particular, you'll learn how to capture the nuances of sunrise and magic-hour light. Marco can work with all types of camera, tailor tours to personal interests and arrange photography trips round the lagoon.

Eating

Ristorante Quadri

ITALIAN **€€€**

When it comes to Venetian glamour, nothing beats this historic Michelin-starred restaurant overlooking Piazza San Marco. A swarm of waiters greets you as you're shown to your table in a room decked out with silk damask, gilt, painted beams and Murano chandeliers. Dishes are precise and delicious, deftly incorporating Venetian touches into an inventive modern Italian menu. (www.alajmo.it)

Bistrot de Venise

VENETIAN **€€€**

12 MAP P52, F3

Indulge in some culinary time travel in the red-and-gilt dining room at this fine-dining bistro reviving the recipes of Renaissance chef Bartolomeo Scappi. Dine like a doge on braised duck with wild apple and onion pudding, or enjoy the Jewish recipe of goose, raisin and pine-nut pasta. Desserts such as *panna cotta* with lavender honey are beguilingly exotic. (www.bistrotdevenise.com)

Trattoria Da Fiore VENETIAN €€€

13 MAP P52, C4

Rustic-chic decor sets the scene for excellent Venetian dishes composed of carefully selected seasonal ingredients from small Veneto producers. The restaurant is justly famous for its seafood dishes. Next door, the bar's *cicheti* counter serves tasty snacks at more democratic prices. (www.dafiore.it)

Suso GELATO €

14 MAP P52, F2

Suso's gelati are locally made and free of artificial colours. Indulge in rich, original seasonal flavours such as marscapone cream with fig sauce and walnuts. Vegan gelati and gluten-free cones are available. (www.gelatovenezia.it)

Ai Mercanti ITALIAN €€

15 MAP P52, E3

With its pumpkin-coloured walls, gleaming golden fixtures and jet-black tables and chairs, Ai Mercanti effortlessly conjures up a romantic mood. No wonder diners whisper over glasses of wine selected from the vast list before tucking into modern bistro-style dishes. Although there's a focus on seafood and secondary cuts of meat, there are some wonderful vegetarian options as well, and you can sit alfresco on tiny Corte Coppo. (www.aimercanti.it)

Marchini Time BAKERY €

16 MAP P52, E3

Elbow your way through the morning crush to bag a warm croissant filled with runny apricot jam or melting Nutella. Everything here is freshly baked, which is why the crowd hangs around as croissants give way to focaccia, *pizzette* (mini pizzas) and generously stuffed *panini*. Their gorgeous marzipan mini fruits make a great gift. (www.marchinitime.it)

Osteria da Carla VENETIAN €€

17 MAP P52, F4

Diners in the know duck into this hidden courtyard, less than 100m from Piazza San Marco, to snack on *cicheti* at the counter or to sit down to a romantic meal. The surroundings are at once modern and ancient, with exposed brick and contemporary artworks. (www.osteriadacarla.it)

Rosa Salva BAKERY €

18 MAP P52, F3

With just-baked strudel and reliable cappuccino, Rosa Salva has provided Venetians with fresh reasons to roll out of bed for more than a century. Cheerfully efficient women working the spotless counter supply gale-force espresso and turbo-loaded pistachio profiteroles to power you across 30 more bridges. Come lunchtime, the sweet pastries are replaced by plump sandwiches and hot deli plates. (www.rosasalva.it)

Rosticceria Gislon DELI €

19 MAP P52, F2

Serving San Marco workers since the 1930s, this no-frills *rosticceria* (roast-meat specialist) has an ultramarine canteen counter downstairs and a small eat-in restaurant upstairs. For a quick bite you'll find *arancini* (rice balls), deep-fried mozzarella, croquettes and fish fry-ups. No one said it was going to be healthy!

Drinking

Grancaffè Quadri CAFE

20 MAP P52, G4

This baroque bar-cafe has been serving happy hours since 1638. During Carnevale, costumed Quadri revellers party like it's 1699 – despite prices shooting up to €15 for a *spritz*. Grab a seat on the piazza to watch the best show in town: the basilica's golden mosaics ablaze in the sunset. (www.alajmo.it)

Bar Longhi COCKTAIL BAR

21 MAP P52, D6

Gritti Palace's beautiful Bar Longhi may be pricey, but if you consider your surrounds – Fortuny fabrics,

Grancaffè Quadri

IVANCHIK/SHUTTERSTOCK ©

Venetian Wells

'Venetia è in acqua, et non ha acqua,' wrote 15th-century Venetian historian Marino Sudo: 'Venice is on the water, and it has no water.' Fresh water was hard to come by in the briny paradise Venetians chose as their shelter, so they devised a system to collect rain. They designed their *campi* (squares) with a slant to let water gather in tanks right in the middle – the Venetian wells. At the peak of this system, Venice counted as many as 2000 wells, though today only 600 are left in either public or private hands. Over time, wells became a form of art and a way to record ownership and events.

In San Marco – a *sestiere* (district) known for its grandeur – it's wells that I like to visit the most. In Campo S Anzolo a well testifies the donation of the Santa Maria Annunziata Oratory, built by the powerful Morosini family in 920 and dedicated to the Archangel Gabriel and to the brotherhood of the Zoti, the 'limp ones', devoted to celebrating the Assumption of the Virgin Mary. And there they both are – on one side of the well's belly Gabriel carries a lily to the Virgin Mary, who kneels in prayer on the other side.

Near Calle delle Mercerie, a well with two engraved cats honours the Menor dalla Gatta family (*gatta* meaning cat), who gifted the well for public use. Those two cats, lazily playing with a ball, encapsulate much of the Venetian spirit: art and playfulness in harmony. Venetians call the marble body of the well *vera*, or 'wedding ring,' as if Venice wanted to woo those invisible pockets of fresh water, their 2000 liquid vows.

Recommended by Marina Dora Martino,
a poet living in Venice,
@mm_doppiaemme

18th-century mirrors, an intarsia marble bar and million-dollar Pietro Longhi paintings – the price of a signature orange martini starts to seem reasonable. In summer you'll have to choose between the twinkling interior and a spectacular Grand Canal terrace. (www.hotelgrittipalacevenice.com)

Harry's Bar

BAR

22 MAP P52, F5

Aspiring auteurs sit at tables well scuffed by Ernest Hemingway, Charlie Chaplin, Truman Capote and Orson Welles at this compact 1930s bar. Enjoy the signature €22 Bellini (Giuseppe Cipriani's original 1948 recipe: white peach juice and prosecco) with a side of reflected glory. (www.cipriani.com)

L'Ombra del Leoni

BAR

23 MAP P52, F5

Take in Palazzo Ca' Giustinian's peerless waterside Grand Canal position in this cafe-restaurant. Try to nab a seat on the outdoor terrace – it's the perfect spot to watch the gondolas come and go against a backdrop of basilicas.

Teamo

WINE BAR

24 MAP P52, D4

By day this is more of a cafe, serving asymmetrical plates of pasta, but in the evening its little tables fill up with a mixed crowd, drinking wine and snacking on massive platters of *salumi* (cured meats) and cheese. (www.teamowinebar.com)

Enoteca al Volto

WINE BAR

25 MAP P52, D3

Join the punters working their way through the vast selection of plump *cicheti* in this historic wood-panelled bar that feels like the inside of a ship's hold. Lining the ceiling above the golden glow of the brass bar lanterns are hundreds of wine labels from just some of the bottles of regional wines that are cracked open every night. (http://enotecaalvolto.com)

Black-Jack

WINE BAR

26 MAP P52, E3

Charming staff dispense delicious *cicheti* from a central bar shaped

Harry's Bar

Keeping Venice Afloat

Impossible though it seems, Venetians built their home on 117 small islands connected by some 400 bridges over 150 canals. But if floating marble palaces boggle the mind, consider what's underneath them: an entire forest's worth of petrified wood pylons, rammed through silty *barene* (shoals) into the clay lagoon floor.

High Tides

Venice is ingeniously constructed to contend with lagoon tides, so even a four-alarm *acqua alta* (exceptionally high tide) is rarely cause for panic. But on 4 November 1966, record floods poured into 16,000 Venetian homes in terrifying waves, and residents were stranded in the wreckage of 1400 years of civilisation. Thanks to Venice's international appeal, assistance poured in and Unesco coordinated 50 private organisations to redress the ravages of the deluge. In 2019 another flood, only 7cm short of the 1966 one, caused intensive damage, including to the mosaic floors of the Basilica di San Marco.

Cleaning up after *acqua alta* is a tedious job for Venetians: pumping water out of flooded ground floors and preventing corrosion by scrubbing salt residue off surfaces. Venice's canals must also be regularly dredged, which involves pumping water out, removing pungent sludge, then patching brickwork by hand with a ticklish technique Venetians call *scuci-cuci*.

Environmental Challenges

Venice and its lagoon are a World Heritage site – but in the wake of Tuscany's 2012 Costa Concordia shipwreck, Unesco expressed concern about the impact of cruise ships and unsustainable tourism. Locally, opposition to cruise ships was led by critics such as No Grandi Navi (No Big Ships), which spearheaded a successful campaign to have them banned from the lagoon. This eventually came in August 2021 when the Italian government barred vessels weighing more than 25,000 tonnes from entering the lagoon.

Meanwhile, responsible travellers are taking action – arriving by train not plane; eating sustainably sourced, local food; conserving water; using products free of industrial chemicals; and supporting local businesses to help offset tourism impact and keep Venice afloat.

like a horseshoe in this gleaming marble-floored little place in the main shopping precinct. It's a great place for a snack and a tipple on your way to La Fenice or Teatro Goldoni; you could easily make a meal of it.

Entertainment

Teatro La Fenice OPERA

27 MAP P52, D4

One of Italy's top opera houses, glamorous La Fenice stages a rich roster of opera, ballet and classical music. The main opera season runs from January to July and September to October. The cheapest seats (€15) are in the boxes at the top: the view is extremely restricted, but you will get to hear the music, watch the orchestra, soak up the atmosphere and people-watch. Built in glitteringly lavish 19th-century style, La Fenice (the Phoenix) has burnt down three times, most recently in 1996 as a result of an arson attack. (www.teatrolafenice.it)

Teatro Goldoni THEATRE

28 MAP P52, E3

Named after the city's great playwright, Carlo Goldoni, Venice's main theatre has an impressive dramatic range that runs from Goldoni's comedy to Shakespearean tragedy (mostly in Italian), plus ballets and concerts. Don't be fooled by the huge 20th-century bronze doors: this venerable theatre dates from 1622, and the jewel-box interior seats just 800. (www.teatrostabileveneto.it)

Teatro Goldoni

Wagner Says 'Shhhh!'

By the 19th century, Venice's great families were largely ruined and could not afford to heat their enormous *palazzi*. Instead, aristocrats would spend much of the day at La Fenice (p63), which served as a members-only club, where they could gamble, gossip and provide running commentary during performances. When he first performed at La Fenice, German composer Richard Wagner miffed the notoriously chatty Venetian opera crowd by insisting on total silence during performances.

Shopping

Chiarastella Cattana

HOMEWARES

29 MAP P52, B4

Transform any home with these locally woven, strikingly original Venetian linens. Whimsical cushions feature chubby purple rhinoceroses and grumpy scarlet elephants straight out of Pietro Longhi paintings, and hand-tasselled jacquard hand towels will dry your guests in style. Decorators and design aficionados should save an afternoon to consider dizzying woven-to-order napkin and curtain options. (www.chiarastellacattana.com)

Atelier Segalin di Daniela Ghezzo

SHOES

30 MAP P52, E4

A gold chain pulled across this historic atelier doorway means Daniela is already consulting with a client, discussing rare leathers while taking foot measurements. Each pair of shoes is custom-made, so you'll never see your fabric Venetian platform shoes on another diva, or your dimpled manta-ray brogues on a rival mogul. Expect to pay around €1000 and wait six weeks for delivery. (www.danielaghezzo.it)

L'Armadio di Coco Luxury Vintage

VINTAGE

31 MAP P52, D5

Jam-packed with pre-loved designer treasures from yesteryear, this tiny shop is the place to come for classic Chanel dresses, exquisite cashmere coats and limited-edition Gucci shoulder bags. (www.larmadiodicoco.it)

L'Isola

GLASS

32 MAP P52, B4

Backlit chalices and spotlit vases emit an otherworldly glow at this shrine to Murano modernist glass master Carlo Moretti, among other 20th-century craftspeople. Strict shapes contain freeform swirls of orange and red, and glasses etched with fish-scale patterns add wit and a wink to high-minded modernism. (www.lisola.com)

Fortuny

FASHION & ACCESSORIES

33 MAP P52, D5

Get that 'just got in from Monaco for my art opening' look beloved of cashed-up bohemians. The finely pleated Delphos tunic dresses make anyone look like a high-maintenance modern dancer or heiress (Isadora Duncan and Peggy Guggenheim were both fans), and the hand-stamped silk-velvet bags are more arty than ostentatious. (www.fortuny.shop)

Ottica Carraro

FASHION & ACCESSORIES

34 MAP P52, D4

Lost your sunglasses on the Lido? Never fear: Ottica Carraro can make you a custom pair within 24 hours, including the eye exam. The store has its own limited-edition 'Venice' line, ranging from cat-eye shades perfect for facing paparazzi to chunky wood-grain frames that could get you mistaken for an art critic at the Biennale. (www.otticacarraro.it)

Camuffo

GLASS

35 MAP P52, F3

Kids, entomologists and glass collectors seek out Signor Camuffo in this cabinet of miniature natural wonders. Expect to find him wielding a blowtorch as he fuses metallic foils and molten glass into shimmering wings for the city's finest lamp-worked glass beetles and dragonflies. Between bugs, he'll chat about his work and sell you strands of Murano glass beads.

Cushions, Fortuny

Explore

Dorsoduro & the Accademia

Dorsoduro covers prime Grand Canal waterfront with Ca' Rezzonico's golden-age splendour, the Peggy Guggenheim Collection's modern edge, Gallerie dell'Accademia's Renaissance beauties and Punta della Dogana's ambitious installation art. Locals laze days away on the water's edge at Zattere, and convene in Campo Santa Margherita for spritz and banter. While the eastern tip is heavily touristy, the area develops a more local feel the further west you go.

The Short List

- ***Gallerie dell'Accademia (p68)*** *Getting a crash course in Venetian art at this historic gallery*
- ***Peggy Guggenheim Collection (p72)*** *Schmoozing with Picasso, Pollock and other greats of modern art.*
- ***Basilica di Santa Maria della Salute (p78)*** *Marvelling at mystical architecture and finding hidden Titian masterpieces.*
- ***Ca' Rezzonico (p78)*** *Waltzing through baroque ballrooms, salons and boudoirs decked in sublime art.*
- ***Punta della Dogana (p78)*** *Comparing fearless contemporary art amid boldly repurposed architecture.*

Getting There & Around

Vaporetto Grand Canal 1, 2 and N lines stop at Accademia; line 1 also calls at Ca' Rezzonico and Salute. Lines 5.1, 5.2, 6 and the N (night) stop at the Zattere and/or San Basilio.

Traghetto A gondola ferry crosses the Grand Canal to San Marco from the Basilica di Santa Maria della Salute.

Dorsoduro & the Accademia Map on p76

Basilica di Santa Maria della Salute (p78)

Top Experience

Admire Art at Gallerie dell'Accademia

Hardly academic, these galleries contain more murderous intrigue, forbidden romance and shameless politicking than the most outrageous Venetian parties. For centuries the Scuola della Carità complex containing the galleries housed religious orders, but ever since Napoleon installed his haul of Venetian art trophies here in 1807 – mainly looted from various religious institutions – there's been nonstop visual drama inside these walls.

MAP P76, E4

www.gallerieaccademia.it

The Building

The Accademia inhabits three conjoined buildings. The **Scuola della Carità** (founded 1260) was the oldest of Venice's six *scuole grandi* (religious confraternities); the current building dates from 1343. Bartolomeo Bon completed the spare, Gothic-edged facade of the **Chiesa di Santa Maria della Carità** in 1448. A century later, Palladio took a classical approach to the **Convento dei Canonici Lateranensi**. From 1949 to 1954, Carlo Scarpa chose a minimalist approach to restorations.

The bulk of the collection's treasures are on the 1st floor, and this is the best place to start your visit. The ground floor houses major exhibitions, sculpture and a less showstopping collection of paintings from 1600 to 1880.

Looking into the Past

Floor plans help you pick out your favourite Renaissance genius painters. But also be prepared to follow your eyes as you look into the past and lock your gaze with **Lorenzo Lotto**'s soul-searching *Portrait of a Young Scholar*, **Rosalba Carriera**'s brutally honest self-portrait and **Pietro Longhi**'s lovestruck violinist in *The Dance Lesson*.

Sensory Overload

Take the stairs up from the grand entry hall and prepare to be overwhelmed by the sensory overload of Room 1, where a swarm of angels flutter their golden wings from the **carved ceiling**, gazing down upon a swirling polychrome marble floor. Competing valiantly for your attention are a collection of vivid 14th- and 15th-century religious works that show Venice's precocious flair for colour and drama.

★ Top Tips

- To skip ahead of the queues in high season, book tickets in advance online (booking fee €1.50).
- Queues are shorter in the afternoon; last entry is 45 minutes before closing, but a proper visit takes at least 1½ hours.
- The audio guide is mostly descriptive and largely unnecessary – avoid the wait and follow your bliss and the explanatory wall tags.
- Bags larger than 20cm by 30cm by 15cm need to be stored in the lockers, which require a refundable €1 coin.

Take a Break

Impoverished artists and gallery-goers descend on Bar alla Toletta (p82) for grilled-to-order *panini*.

The Artworks

This outstanding collection of artworks is arranged chronologically, with the earliest in Room 1, notably **Paolo Veneziano**'s *Coronation of the Virgin Polyptych*, still gleaming bright after nearly 700 years.

In Room 2, **Cima da Conegliano**'s *Incredulity of Saint Thomas and Saint Magnus of Oderzo* contrasts the symmetrical elegance of the architecture surrounding the figures of the saints and the risen Christ with the electric human drama of their recognition. A sombre and absorbing **Bellini** altarpiece (Room 3) shows a sadly suffering Christ gently enclosed by the hovering wings of stylishly robed angels.

In Room 4 you'll see a small, solemnly absorbing work by **Piero della Francesca** – one of the few he signed – depicting St Jerome in a rustic tunic, pausing his reading to greet a devotee (a vivid portrait of the man who commissioned the painting). In the same room, **Andrea Mantegna**'s *San Giorgio* strikes a fetching pose in natty armour, the green dragon dead at his feet.

Hieronymus Bosch startles in Room 7 with an image of a woman hanging from a cross, albeit a faintly bearded woman. She has been identified as Saint Wilgefortis, crucified by her father when she miraculously grew a beard to avoid an arranged marriage.

Paolo Veronese's restored *Feast in the House of Levi* (Room 10) was originally called *Last Supper*, until Inquisition leaders condemned it for showing dogs and drunkards, among others, cavorting with Apostles.

Ceiling of Sala dell'Albergo

Veronese refused to change a thing besides the title. In his huge *Crucifixion* in the same room, dark storm clouds gather overhead, and a demon bursts out of the ground, causing a foreground horse to rear up and cast the rider backwards.

Titian's 1576 *Pietà* (Room 11) was possibly finished posthumously by Palma il Giovane, but notice the smears of paint Titian applied with his bare hands and the column-base self-portrait. Room 19 holds the delightfully named **Boccaccio Boccaccino**'s *Mystic Marriage of Saint Catherine with Saints Rosa, Peter, John the Baptist, the Annunciation to the Shepherds, the Flight into Egypt, and the Magi on Horseback*: a lot of drama presented with restrained grace.

Room 20 is full of large canvases taken from the Scuola Grande di San Giovanni Evangelista (p102). **Gentile Bellini**'s *Procession in Piazza San Marco* offers an intriguing view of Venice's most famous square before its 16th-century makeover, while the former wooden version of the city's most famous bridge appears in **Vittore Carpaccio**'s *Miracle of the Relic of the Cross at Rialto Bridge*. Venetian Renaissance master **Tintoretto**'s *Creation of the Animals* (Room 23) is a fantastical bestiary, suggesting God put forth his best efforts inventing Venetian seafood (no argument here).

The **Sala dell'Albergo** (Room 24) has been left untouched from when it was the Scuola della Carità's boardroom. Meetings would not have been boring here, under a lavishly carved ceiling (pictured left and on p68) and facing **Antonio Vivarini**'s *Madonna Enthroned with Child in the Heavenly Garden*, filled with fluffy-bearded saints. **Titian** closes the 1st-floor circuit with his touching *Presentation of the Virgin*. Here, a young, tiny Madonna ringed by heavenly light trudges up an intimidating staircase while a distinctly Venetian crowd of onlookers point at her.

Top Experience

Visit the Palatial Peggy Guggenheim Collection

American heiress Peggy Guggenheim befriended Dadaists, dodged Nazis and changed art history at her palatial home on the Grand Canal. Her Palazzo Venier dei Leoni is a showcase for surrealism, futurism and abstract expressionism by some 200 breakthrough modern artists, including Peggy's second husband Max Ernst and Jackson Pollock (one of her rumoured lovers).

MAP P76, F5

www.guggenheim-venice.it

Modernist Collection

Peggy Guggenheim escaped Paris two days before the Nazi invasion, and boldly defied established social and artistic dictates. She collected according to her own convictions, featuring folk art and lesser-known female artists alongside such radical early modernists as Kandinsky, Picasso, Man Ray, Rothko, Mondrian, Joseph Cornell and Dalí.

Italian Avant-Garde

Upon her 1948 arrival in Venice, Peggy became a spirited advocate for contemporary Italian art, which had largely gone out of favour with the rise of Mussolini and the partisan politics of WWII. Her support led to reappraisals of Umberto Boccioni, Giorgio Morandi, Giacomo Balla, Giuseppe Capogrossi and Giorgio de Chirico, and aided Venice's own Emilio Vedova and Giuseppe Santomaso. Peggy gave passing gondoliers an eyeful on her Grand Canal quay: Marino Marini's 1948 *Angel of the City*, a bronze male nude on horseback, throws back his head and arms and reveals his erect penis.

Sculpture Garden

In the sculpture garden, wander past bronzes by Henry Moore, Alberto Giacometti and Constantin Brancusci, Yoko Ono's *Wish Tree* and a shiny black-granite piece by Anish Kapoor. The city granted an honorary dispensation for Peggy to be buried beneath the Giacometti sculptures, alongside her dearly departed lapdogs.

At Home with Peggy

Cubist works by Braque, Picasso and Duchamp break with the tradition of perspective around Peggy's long wooden dining table. And in her bedroom, dainty mini-mobile earrings by Alexander Calder echo his kinetic hanging sculpture in the palazzo's entrance hall.

★ Top Tips

- Excellent audio guides are available in Italian, English, German, French and Spanish.
- Free daily presentations in Italian and English are given on Peggy's life and the works in the collection (11.30am, noon, 3pm, 3.30pm).
- You're required to store your bags in the free lockers near the ticket office.
- Quiz anyone with an 'Ask me about the Art' badge: they're Guggenheim interns in training.
- Free Kids' Day workshops (in Italian) are held on Sundays at 3pm for children aged four to 10.

Take a Break

The gallery's pavilion **cafe** offers excellent espresso, light lunches (with vegan options), high tea and prosecco with views over the sculpture garden.

Walking Tour

Happy Hour in Campo Santa Margherita

By day Campo Santa Margherita hosts a weekday fish market, the odd flea market and periodic political protests, but by six o'clock this unruly square becomes Venice's nightlife hub. Just don't try to pack it all into one happy hour. Pace yourself on your giro d'ombra *(pub crawl), and alternate* spritz *with* aqua minerale.

Walk Facts

Start Bakarò do Draghi; vaporetto Ca' Rezzonico

Finish Orient Experience II; vaporetto Ca' Rezzonico

Length 700m; 25 minutes

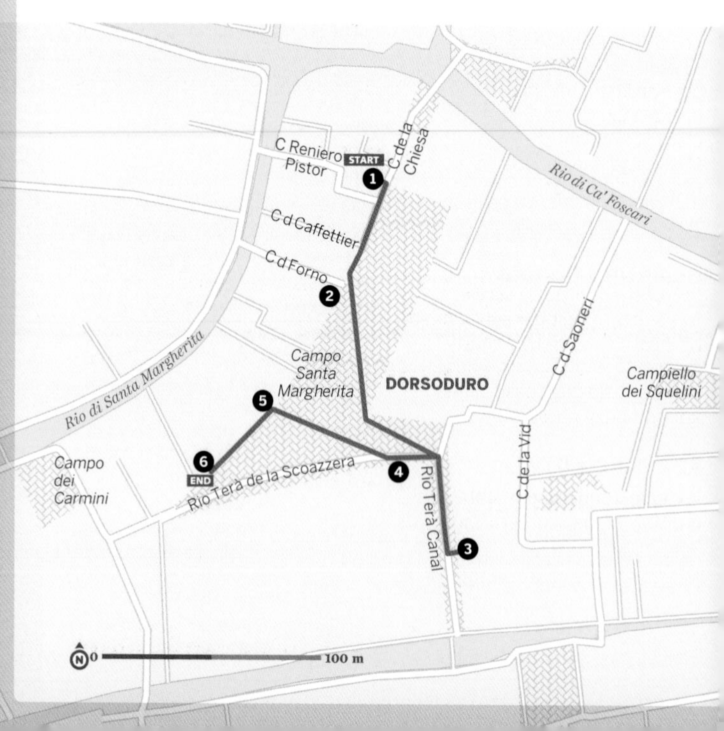

❶ Bakarò

'Permesso!' (pardon!) is the chorus inside this **historic bar**, where the crowd spills onto the pavement and tries not to spill drinks in the process. Arrive at the tiny wooden bar early for the best choice of 45-plus wines by the glass and respectable *tramezzini* (sandwiches).

❷ Il Caffè Rosso

Locals affectionately call this shabby-chic red storefront **Il Rosso** (the red), and its inexpensive *spritz* (prosecco cocktail) generously splashed with scarlet Aperol gives visitors and locals alike an instant flush of Venetian colour. Plan to arrive when the clock strikes '*spritz* o'clock' at 6pm sharp, and mingle with standing-room-only crowds.

❸ Imagina Café

For your next stop, branch out to top-shelf cocktails served at this sleek, backlit **bar** surrounded by local art. A creative, chatty and gay-friendly crowd, whose sweater-clad dogs bask in the admiration of passers-by.

❹ Gelateria Il Doge

If you're wondering what the crowd is at the southern end of the *campo*, it's the mob eyeing up the sumptuous selection of gelato at this venerable **ice-cream parlour** (www.gelateriaildoge.como). Fill your cone with pink Himalayan salt, fig and caramel swirl and Sicilian lemon *granita* (sorbet). Vegan and sugar-free nut or chocolate options make for a virtuous gelato experience.

❺ Osteria alla Bifora

While *spritz*-drinking students carouse outside in the *campo* (square), gentle flirting ensues in this chandelier-lit medieval **wine cave** over big-hearted Veneto merlot. While you wait for a platter of cheese and carved-to-order cured meats to arrive, you'll make new friends at communal tables.

❻ Orient Experience II

Despite its dialogue with the East, Venice lacks good ethnic eateries, but this wildly popular **Eastern deli** aims to set that straight. Run by Ahmed, it fills up colourful bowls with Afghan, Iranian, Turkish and Maghrebi cuisine for hungry students, curious Venetians and travellers in search of vegan fare. Round it all off with a delicious cup of cardamom coffee and some pistachio baklava.

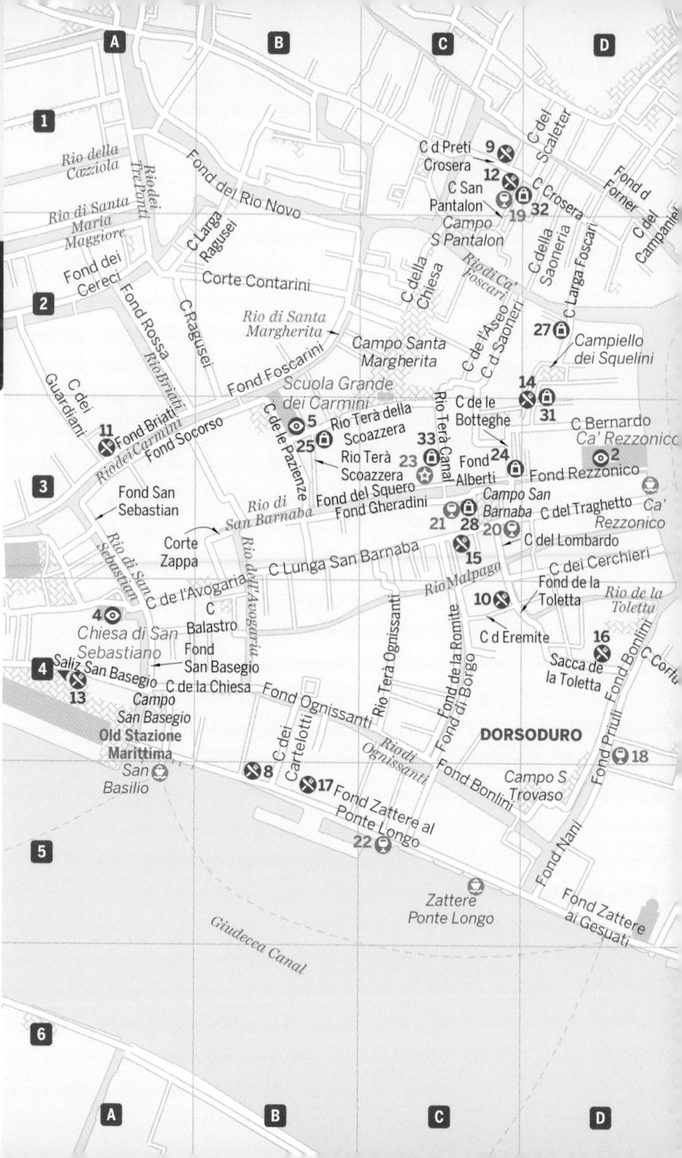

A B C D

1

Rio della Cazziola
Rio dei Tre Ponti
Rio di Santa Maria Maggiore
Fond del Rio Novo
C Larga Ragusei
C d Preti Crosera
9
12
C San Pantalon
19
32
Campo S Pantalon
C del Scaleter
C Crosera
Fond d Forner
C del Campaniel

2

Fond dei Cereci
Fond Rossa
C Ragusei
Corte Contarini
Rio di Santa Margherita
C della Chiesa
Rio di Ca' Foscari
C della Saoneria
C Larga Foscari
C de l'Aseo
C d Saoneri
27
Campiello dei Squelini
Campo Santa Margherita
Fond Foscarini
Rio Briati
C dei Guardiani

3

Scuola Grande dei Carmini
14
31
C de le Botteghe
C Bernardo
Ca' Rezzonico
2
11
Fond Briati
Rio dei Carmini
Fond Socorso
5
C de le Pazienze
Rio Terà della Scoazzera
25
33
Rio Terà Canal
Fond Alberti
24
Fond Rezzonico
Rio Terà Scoazzera
23
Fond del Squero
Fond Gheradini
Campo San Barnaba
21
28
20
C del Traghetto
Ca' Rezzonico
Fond San Sebastian
Rio di San Barnaba
Corte Zappa
Rio di San Sebastian
Rio dell'Avogaria
C Lunga San Barnaba
15
C del Lombardo
C dei Cerchieri
Rio Malpaga
Fond de la Toletta
Rio de la Toletta
10
C de l'Avogaria
C Balastro
4
Chiesa di San Sebastiano
Rio Terà Ognissanti
Fond de la Romite
Fond di Borgo
C d Eremite
16
Sacca de la Toletta
Fond Bonlini
C Cortu

4

Fond San Basegio
Saliz San Basegio
13
C de la Chiesa
Fond Ognissanti
Campo San Basegio
Old Stazione Marittima
San Basilio
C dei Cartelotti
Rio di Ognissanti
DORSODURO
Fond Priuli
18
8
17
Fond Bonlini
Campo S Trovaso
Fond Zattere al Ponte Longo
22

5

Fond Nani
Zattere Ponte Longo
Fond Zattere ai Gesuati
Giudecca Canal

6

A B C D

E F G H

0 200 m
0 0.1 miles

1

Sant'Angelo
San Tomà
Grand Canal
Rio di Ca' Santi
Corte dell'Albero
Rio di Sant'Angelo
C Pesaro
C dei Avvocati
C de la Mandola

2

C Mocenigo Ca' Vecchia
Piscina S Samuele
Rio de la Verona
C de la Verona
Rio dei Barcaroli
C d Caffettier
Campo S Anzolo
San Samuele
C de le Carrozze
C de le Botteghe
C dei Frati
Saliz Malipiero
C Caotorta
C de la Fenice
C dei Orbi
SAN MARCO
Ramo Primo dei Calegheri

3

C del Spezier
Rio de la Veste
C Veste
Campo di San Moisè
Campo Santo Stefano
Fond de la Malvasia Vecchia
Campo S Maurizio
Fond Corner Zaguri
C Larga XXII Marzo
Rio del Duca
C Vitturi
C Giustinian
C de le Ostreghe
Campo di S Vidal
Campo di Santa Maria del Giglio
C del Traghetto
Corte Barozzi
Ponte dell'Accademia
Rio dell'Orso
C del Dose da Ponte
Rio di San Maurizio
C Gritti
Campo Traghetto

4

Campo de la Carità
Rio Terà Carità
Gallerie dell'Accademia
Peggy Guggenheim Collection
Santa Maria del Giglio Traghetto
Fond Dogana alla Salute
Punta della Dogana
Salute
Palazzo Cini
Campo San Vio
Ca' Dario
Campo de la Salute
3
C Larga Pisani
Piscina Forner
6
C S Cristoforo
C d Bastion
1
C d Chiesa
Fond Venier dei Leoni
30
Basilica di Santa Maria della Salute
Rio Terà Antonio Foscarini
Piscina Venier
29
C Bragadin
Fond Ospedaleto
26
Rio Terà Catecumeni

5

C Franchi
Fond Venier
Fond de Ca' Bragadin
C Molin
Fond Soranzo de la Fornace
Rio de la Salute
Fond Zattere ai Saloni
Piscina S Agnese
C d Squero
Rio Terà San Vio
Fond di Ca' Balà
C da Ponte
Rio di San Vio
Rio de le Torselle
C degli Incurabili
Fondazione Vedova
7
Fond Zattere Santo Spirito
Alilaguna
Rio de le Fornace

6

E F G H

Sights

Basilica di Santa Maria della Salute

BASILICA

1 MAP P76, H5

Baldassare Longhena's magnificent basilica is prominently positioned near the entrance to the Grand Canal, its white stones, exuberant statuary and high domes gleaming spectacularly. The church makes good on an official appeal by the Venetian Senate to the Madonna in 1630, after 80,000 Venetians had been killed by plague. Titian masterpieces deck out the Sacristry, while life in a time of plague is a miracle worth celebrating in Tintoretto's upbeat *Wedding Feast of Cana*, featuring a Venetian throng of multicultural musicians and Tintoretto himself, depicted with a long beard near the bottom left of the canvas. (www.basilicasalutevenezia.it)

Ca' Rezzonico

Ca' Rezzonico

MUSEUM

2 MAP P76, D3

Baroque dreams come true at this Baldassare Longhena–designed Grand Canal *palazzo* (mansion), where a marble staircase leads to a vast gilded **ballroom** and sumptuous salons filled with period furniture, paintings, porcelain and mesmerising ceiling frescoes, four of which were painted by Giambattista Tiepolo. The building was largely stripped of finery when the Rezzonico family departed in 1810, but this was put right after the city acquired it in 1935, and refurnished it with pieces salvaged from other decaying palaces. (www.visitmuve.it)

Punta della Dogana

GALLERY

3 MAP P76, H5

Fortuna, the weathervane atop Punta della Dogana, swung Venice's way in 2005, when bureaucratic hassles in Paris convinced art collector François Pinault to showcase his works in Venice's long-abandoned customs warehouses. Built by Giuseppe Benoni in 1677 to ensure no ship entered the Grand Canal without paying duties, the warehouses reopened in 2009 after a striking reinvention by Japanese architect Tadao Ando. The space now hosts exhibitions of ambitious, large-scale artworks from contemporary art stars. (www.palazzograssi.it)

Chiesa di San Sebastiano

CHURCH

4 MAP P76, A4

Antonio Scarpignano's relatively austere 1508–48 facade creates a sense of false modesty at this neighbourhood church. The interior is adorned with floor-to-ceiling masterpieces by Paolo Veronese, executed over three decades. According to popular local legend, Veronese found sanctuary at San Sebastiano in 1555 after fleeing murder charges in Verona, and his works in this church deliver lavish thanks to the parish and an especially brilliant poke in the eye of his accusers. (www.chorusvenezia.org)

Scuola Grande dei Carmini

HISTORIC BUILDING

5 MAP P76, B3

Seventeenth-century backpackers must have thought they'd died and gone to heaven at this magnificent confraternity clubhouse, dedicated to Our Lady of Mt Carmel, with its lavish interiors by Giambattista Tiepolo and Baldassare Longhena. Leading up from the unusual monochrome frescoes by Niccolò Bambini, the gold-leafed, Longhena-designed stucco stairway heads up towards Tiepolo's nine-panel ceiling of a rosy *Virgin in Glory*. The adjoining hostel room is bedecked in marble and *boiserie* (wood carving). (www.scuolagrande carmini.it)

Sacred Music at Salute

If you think the Longhena-designed dome of the **Basilica di Santa Maria della Salute** looks magnificent, wait until you hear how it sounds. Weekdays at 3.30pm, vespers are played on the basilica's organ, dating from 1783. These musical interludes are free, and the acoustics are nothing short of celestial.

Palazzo Cini

GALLERY

6 MAP P76, F5

This elegant 16th-century Gothic *palazzo* is the former home of industrialist and philanthropist Vittorio Cini, who filled it with first-class paintings, period furnishings, ceramics and Murano glass. Wonderful paintings by lesser-known Renaissance lights such as Filippo Lippi, Piero di Cosimo and Dosso Dossi cover the walls, their glowing brilliance having even more impact in these intimate, domestic spaces. (www.palazzocini.it)

Fondazione Vedova

GALLERY

7 MAP P76, G6

A retrofit designed by Pritzker Prize–winning architect Renzo Piano transformed Venice's historic salt warehouses into art galleries. Although the facade is from the 1830s, the warehouses were established in the 14th century, when the all-important salt monopoly secured Venice's fortune. The repurposing of the buildings is only fitting, now that the city's most precious commodity is art. They're only open for exhibitions staged by the foundation formed in honour of Venetian painter Emilio Vedova. (www.fondazionevedova.org)

Eating

Riviera ITALIAN €€€

8 MAP P76, B5

Former rock musician GP Cremonini founded this top-end restaurant – Dorsoduro's finest – which delivers exemplary service and perfectly cooked seafood: think homemade pasta with scallops or sea bass poached with prawns. The setting, overlooking the Giudecca Canal, is similarly spectacular. For serious gourmands, the 11-course tasting menu with wine pairings is an unmissable experience. (www.ristorante riviera.it)

Estro INTERNATIONAL €€

9 MAP P76, C1

Estro is anything you want it to be: wine bar, *aperitivo* (pre-dinner drink) pit stop or sit-down degustation restaurant. The vast selection of wine was chosen by young-gun owners Alberto and Dario, whose passion for quality extends to the food – from *baccalà mantecato* (creamed cod) on polenta crisps, to guinea-fowl lasagne or a succulent burger dripping with Asiago cheese. (www.estrovenezia.com)

Enoteca ai Artisti ITALIAN €€€

10 MAP P76, C4

Dishes from the daily changing menu might include a lightly curried rabbit *maltagliati* (cut pasta) or beef cheeks with polenta chips at this elegant *enoteca* (wine-orientated bistro), paired with exceptional wines by the glass. Sidewalk tables are great for people-watching, but book ahead as space is limited inside and out. Note: only turf (no surf) dishes on Mondays, as the fish market is closed. (www.enotecaartisti.com)

Da Codroma VENETIAN €€

11 MAP P76, A3

In a city plagued by high prices and indifferent eating, the shared wooden tables and waterside seats at Da Codroma are the antidote. Chef Nicola faithfully maintains Venetian traditions here, serving up *il saor* (cured sardines and prawns), *bigoli in salsa* (buckwheat pasta with anchovy and onions) and delicious semifreddo to locals and savvy tourists alike. (www.facebook.com/dacodroma)

Pasticceria Tonolo PASTRIES €

12 MAP P76, C1

Long, skinny Tonolo is the stuff of local legend. Ditch packaged B&B croissants for bargain flaky apple strudel, velvety *bignè al zabaione* (marsala cream pastry) and oozing chocolate croissants. Devour your pastry or *pizzetta* (small pizza)at the bar, and wash it down with coffee served in dainty china cups. (http:/pasticceria-tonolo-venezia.business.site)

La Tecia Vegana

VEGAN €

13 MAP P76, A4

Located off the tourist map in a studenty district, Venice's only organic vegan restaurant serves delectable dishes such as tempeh *mafè* (peanut butter sauce) with rice. But its real triumph is to successfully mimic a classic Italian menu, with *primi* such as porcini ravioli, *secondi* including *melanzane Parmigiana* (eggplant Parmigiana) and succulent vegan tiramisu to finish. Many dishes are gluten-free. (www.lateciavegana.com)

Do Farai

VENETIAN €€

14 MAP P76, D3

Venetian regulars pack this crimson wood-panelled room, decorated with Regata Storica victory pendants and Murano glass decanters. The mixed antipasto is a succulent prologue to classic Venetian dishes like pasta with shellfish, grilled *orata* (bream), *fegato alla veneziana* (veal liver with onions on polenta) and *sarde in saor* (sardines in a tangy onion marinade).

La Bitta

VENETIAN €€

15 MAP P76, C3

Venice is known for its seafood but this cosy, green-shuttered bistro taps into the other side of the

Food display in cafe window

Ghostly Venice

Handsomely sited on the Grand Canal, **Ca' Dario** (Map p76, G5) is a 15th-century palazzo with three levels of arched windows abutted by three oculi surrounded by disks of coloured marble. Its mesmerising reflection was once painted by Claude Monet, but it's famous for a more nefarious reason: starting with the daughter of its original owner, Giovanni Dario, an unusual number of its occupants have met untimely deaths and financial ruin. Gossips claim this effectively dissuaded Woody Allen from buying the house in the late 1990s. The former manager of The Who, Kit Lambert, moved out after complaining of being hounded by the palace's ghosts, and was found dead shortly after in 1981. One week after renting the place for a holiday in 2002, The Who's bass player, John Entwhistle, died of a heart attack. Look for it just past the first small canal to the left of the Guggenheim.

cuisine, serving a concise menu focused on meat and seasonal veggies. It's one of the best places in town to try the classic *fegato alla veneziana* (veal liver with onions). Reservations recommended; cash only.

Toletta Snack-Bar SANDWICHES €

16 MAP P76, D4

Midway through museum crawls from Accademia to Ca' Rezzonico, Toletta satisfies those on a budget with lip-smacking, grilled-to-order *panini* (sandwiches), including *prosciutto crudo* (dry-cured ham), rocket and mozzarella, and daily vegetarian options. The *tramezzini* (triangular stacked sandwiches) are tasty too. Get yours to go, or grab a seat for around €1 more.

Oke PIZZA €€

17 MAP P76, B5

This pizzeria entices not for its knock-out cuisine – though the pizzas are more than serviceable – but for its gorgeous watery Zattere location. It's all about the outside tables, with waiters flitting between them toting wheels of pizza, and individual table lamps lighting up your night. Black pizzas infused with squid ink add culinary drama, and celiacs are catered for with an entire gluten-free menu. (https://okevenezia.com)

Drinking

Cantine del Vino già Schiavi VENETIAN €

18 MAP P76, D4

It may look like a wine shop and function as a bar, but this legendary canalside spot also serves the best *cicheti* (Venetian tapas) on this side of the Grand Canal. Choose from the impressive counter selection or ask for a filled-to-order roll. Chaos cheerfully prevails, with an eclectic cast of locals inside, or propping up the canal wall outside. (www.cantinaschiavi.com)

El Sbarlefo

BAR

19 MAP P76, C1

If you're looking to escape the raucous student scene on Campo Santa Margherita, head to this chic bar with its sophisticated soundtrack, high-quality *cicheti* and live music on the weekends. Aside from the long list of regional wines, there's a serious selection of spirits here. (www.elsbarlefo.it)

Ai Artisti

BAR

20 MAP P76, C3

True to its name, artsy student types pack out this engagingly low-key cafe-bar on the weekends and spill out onto the street outside. It's been serving drinks and snacks since 1897, and retains a local feel – as well as affordable *spritzes* and negronis – despite the city's shifting demographics.

Osteria ai Pugni

BAR

21 MAP P76, C3

Centuries ago, brawls on the bridge out the front inevitably ended in the canal, but now Venetians settle differences with one of over 50 wines by the glass at this ever-packed bar, pimped

Ca' Dario (on right)

with recycled Magnum-bottle lamps and wine-crate tables. The latest drops are listed on the blackboard, with *aperitivo*-friendly nibbles including *polpette* (meatballs) and cured local meats on bread. (www.osteriaaipugni.com)

El Chioschetto BAR

22 MAP P76, C5

There's really no better place to park yourself for *aperitivo* and homemade *piadine* (filled flatbreads) than at this pint-sized kiosk on the Zattere overlooking the Giudecca Canal. Even on frosty spring evenings the tables fill up with a mixed crowd downing cocktails and *spritzes* and watching the spectacular Venetian sunset. In summer, on Wednesday and Saturday evenings, there's live music.

Entertainment

Venice Jazz Club JAZZ

23 MAP P76, C3

Jazz is alive and swinging in Dorsoduro, where the resident VJC Jazz Quartet takes to the stage on Monday, Wednesday and Saturday, while the VJC Latin Jazz & Bossa Nova Quartet takes over on Tuesday and Thursday; shows start at 9pm. The venue closes for August, December, January and much of February. (www.venicejazzclub.com)

Shopping

Ca' Macana ARTS & CRAFTS

24 MAP P76, C3

Glimpse the talents behind the feathered and sparkling Venetian Carnevale masks that impressed Stanley Kubrick so much he ordered several for his final film *Eyes Wide Shut*. Choose your papier-mâché persona from the selection of coquettish courtesan's eye-shades, chequered Casanova disguises and long-nosed plague doctor masks – or decorate your own at Ca' Macana's mask-painting workshops (from €39). They have another beautiful shop close by at Calle del Capeler 3215. (www.camacana.com)

Libreria Marco Polo BOOKS

25 MAP P76, B3

One of the best book shops in the city, with novels and non-fiction titles in English and Italian. Owner Claudio and his team can guide you to books about Venice, green issues and contemporary politics, while the children's section heaves with great titles. Friday evenings will often see a book reading or author meet-and-greet happening in the store. (www.libreriamarcopolo.com)

Claudia Canestrelli ANTIQUES

26 MAP P76, G5

Hand-coloured lithographs of fanciful lagoon fish, 19th-century miniatures of cats dressed as generals, and vintage cufflinks

Navigating Venice

This enigmatic and capricious city is as hard to navigate as it is to understand, but there are a few keys to finding your way around.

Street numbers, ranging up to the thousands, are bafflingly high on the tiniest of alleys. They refer not to individual walkways, but to the entire *sestiere* (district, of which there are six, hence the name), and so the numbering jumps from street to street. Street signs (*nizioleti*, meaning 'little sheets' in Venetian dialect) are traditionally stencilled in black on a white background.

When you are searching for a particular address, this key to Venetian geography may help:

- *Calle* – A typical Venetian street, with houses on either side. The word (pronounced with an 'l' rather than Spanish 'y' sound) comes from Latin for 'path'.
- *Campo* – A square. The word means 'field' in Italian, and though the grass and grazing animals are long gone, the term remains. Venice has just one *piazza* (which is the normal Italian word for square): fabled San Marco.
- *Fondamenta* – A pathway that runs along a canal.
- *Piscina* – A square that was once a body of water.
- *Ramo* – Meaning 'branch', a *ramo* is a little street.
- *Rio* – A Venice waterway. Only large canals are bestowed with the name Canale.
- *Rio tera'* – A walkway where a canal once ran – the water may still run beneath your feet.
- *Ruga* – Meaning 'wrinkle,' though some think it derives from the French *rue* (street).
- *Salizada* – Signifying 'paved' – these were the first paved streets in the city.
- *Sotoportego* – A passageway that burrows into the first storey of a building.
- *Strada* – A term used commonly in other Italian cities, but Venice has only one *strada*: wide and brazen Strada Nova in Cannaregio.

make for charming souvenirs of Venice's past in this walk-in curio cabinet. Collector-artisan Claudia Canestrelli brings back bygone elegance with her unique repurposed antique earrings, including free-form baroque pearls dangling from gilded bronze elephants.

Paolo Olbi

ARTS & CRAFTS

27 MAP P76, D2

Thoughts worth committing to paper deserve Paolo Olbi's keepsake books, albums and stationery, whose fans include Hollywood actors and NYC mayors (ask to see the guestbook). Ordinary journals can't compare to Olbi originals, handmade with heavyweight paper and made with exquisite leather bindings. The watercolour postcards of Venice are great frameable, bargain souvenirs. (www.olbi.atspace.com)

Signor Blum

TOYS

28 MAP P76, C3

Kids and adults will equally adore these nostalgia-inducing handmade wooden puzzles of the Rialto Bridge and grinning wooden ducks. Mobiles made of colourful carved gondola prows would seem equally at home in an arty foyer or in a nursery. And did we mention the Venice-themed clocks? (www.signorblum.com)

Marina e Susanna Sent

GLASS

29 MAP P76, F5

Wearable waterfalls and soap-bubble necklaces are Venice-style signatures, thanks to the Murano-born Sent sisters. Defying centuries-old beliefs that women can't handle molten glass, their minimalist art-glass statement jewellery is featured in museum stores worldwide, from Palazzo Grassi to MoMA. See new collections at this store, their flagship Murano studio or the San Marco

Plague doctor mask, Ca' Macana (p84)

and San Polo branches. (www.marinaesusannasent.com)

Le Fórcole di Saverio Pastor

ARTS & CRAFTS

30 MAP P76, G5

This backlit, sawdust-scattered studio is where Saverio Pastor hand-carves *fórcole*: forked wooden gondola oarlocks, individually designed to match a gondolier's height, weight and movement, so the gondola doesn't rock too hard. Pastor's *fórcole* twist elegantly, striking an easy balance on gondolas and mantelpieces alike. (www.forcole.com)

Danghyra

CERAMICS

31 MAP P76, D2

Spare white bisque cups seem perfect for a Zen tea ceremony, but look inside – that iridescent lilac glaze is pure Carnevale. Danghyra's striking ceramics are hand-thrown in Venice with a magic touch: her platinum-glazed bowls make the simplest pasta dish fit for a modern-day doge. (www.danghyra.com)

Acqua Marea

SHOES

32 MAP P76, D1

Question: how do you maintain a *bella figura* (good impression) when high tides are sloshing around your ankles? The answer can be found at Martina Ranaldo's delightful store, which stocks rubber boots in lemon yellow and floral prints, ingenious two-tone rubber spats, ankle boots with coloured soles and comfortable non-leather walking shoes. (www.facebook.com/acquamarea)

Taking a Traghetto

Hop across the Grand Canal with the locals on the San Marco *traghetto* (passenger gondola), which connects Santa Maria del Giglio, 500m west of Piazza San Marco, to the Basilica di Santa Maria della Salute (San Gregorio stop), saving you a 40-minute walk. It costs €2 each way.

Papuni Art

JEWELLERY

33 MAP P76, C3

Venice artisan Ninfa Salerno gives staid pearl strands a sense of humour with bouncy black rubber, weaves fuchsia rubber discs into glowing UFO necklaces, and embeds Murano glass beads in rubber daisy cocktail rings. (www.papuniart.it)

Explore San Polo & Santa Croce

Heavenly devotion and earthly delights co-exist in these twinned neighbourhoods, where divine art rubs up against the ancient red-light district, now home to artisan workshops and wine bars. Don't miss Titian's glowing Madonna at I Frari and Tintorettos at Scuola Grande di San Rocco. Grand Canal museums showcase fashion and natural history, while island produce fills the Rialto Market.

The Short List

- ***Scuola Grande di San Rocco (p90)*** *Seeing New Testament drama at this opulent confraternity clubhouse covered with Tintoretto's visionary paintings.*
- ***I Frari (p92)*** *Watching Titian's red-hot Madonna light up this soaring Gothic basilica.*
- ***Rialto Market (p94)*** *Working up an appetite over lagoon surf and turf at this abundant food market.*
- ***Ca' Pesaro (p102)*** *Ping-ponging between modern masterpieces and Japanese antiques in an ostentatious Grand Canal palace.*
- ***Scuola Grande di San Giovanni Evangelista (p102)*** *Taking over-the-top interior-design cues from some of Venice's top architects and artists.*

Getting There & Around

Vaporetto For Santa Croce sights, San Stae, served by lines 1 and N, is most convenient. Lines 1 and N also service Rialto-Mercato and San Tomà in San Polo.

Traghetto Use the gondola ferry to hop across the Grand Canal from the Rialto to Cannaregio.

San Polo & Santa Croce Map on p100

San Polo

Top Experience

Tour Tintoretto at Scuola Grande di San Rocco

The paint still looks fresh on the 50 action-packed Tintorettos painted between 1575 and 1587 for this confraternity meeting house, dedicated to St Roch, patron of the plague-stricken. While the 1575–77 plague claimed one-third of Venice's residents, Tintoretto painted nail-biting scenes of looming despair and last-minute redemption, illuminating a survivor's struggle with breathtaking urgency.

MAP P100, B5

www.scuolagrandesanrocco.org

Assembly Hall

Downstairs in the assembly hall are works by Venetian A-list artists including Titian, Giorgione and Tiepolo. But Tintoretto steals the show with the story of the Virgin Mary, starting on the left wall with *Annunciation*, where the angel surprises Mary at her sewing. The cycle ends with a dark, cataclysmic *Assumption* (pictured), unlike Titian's serene version at I Frari (p93).

Sala Grande Superiore

Take the grand **Scarpagnino staircase** to the Sala Grande Superiore, where you may be seized with a powerful instinct to duck, given all the action in the **Old Testament ceiling scenes** – you can almost hear the swoop overhead as a winged angel dives to nourish the ailing prophet in *Elijah Fed by an Angel*. Meanwhile, eerie illumination ominously strikes subjects in dark **New Testament wall scenes**. When Tintoretto painted these scenes, the plague had just taken 50,000 Venetians, and the cause and cure were unknown. With dynamic lines pointing to glimmers of hope on still-distant horizons, Tintoretto created a moving parable for epidemics through the ages.

Sala Albergo

The New Testament cycle ends with the *Crucifixion* in the Sala Albergo, where things suddenly begin to look up – literally. Every Venetian artist who'd survived the plague wanted the commission to paint this building, so Tintoretto cheated a little. Instead of producing sketches like his rival Paolo Veronese, he painted this magnificent *tondo* (ceiling panel) and dedicated it to the saint, knowing that such a gift couldn't be refused, or matched by other artists.

★ Top Tips

- From spring to late autumn, the artworks provide a bewitching backdrop to top-notch classical-music concerts. Check the website for details.
- Grab a mirror to avoid neck strain when you view Tintoretto's ceiling panels in the upstairs halls.
- The feast of St Roch (16 August) is celebrated with a solemn Mass and procession around the Campo San Rocco.

Take a Break

Break for superior gourmet *panini* away from the crowds at Bar Ai Nomboli (p107).

Celebrate Venice's survival against the odds with a post-art cocktail at Il Mercante (p109).

Top Experience

Go Gothic at I Frari

As you've no doubt heard, there's a Titian – make that the Titian – altarpiece at I Frari (the Friary). But the 14th-century Gothic basilica is itself a towering achievement, with a heaven-scraping ceiling, intricate marquetry choir stalls and a succession of grandiose monuments lining its high brick walls. While Canova's pyramidal marble tomb (pictured) appears permanently moonlit, Titian's Assunta seems to shed its own sunlight.

MAP P100, C5

www.basilicadeifrari.it

Assunta

Visitors are inexorably drawn to the front of this cavernous Gothic church by a 6.7m by 3.4m altarpiece that seems to glow from within. This is Titian's 1518 *Assunta* (Assumption), capturing the split second the radiant Madonna reaches heavenward, finds her footing on a cloud, and escapes this mortal coil in a dramatic swirl of red and blue robes. Both inside and outside the painting, onlookers gasp and point at the glorious, glowing sight. Titian outdid himself here, upstaging even his own 1526 Pesaro altarpiece – a dreamlike composite family portrait of the *Madonna and Child* with the Venetian Pesaro family. You'll find it on the fourth altar on the left nave.

Other Masterpieces

As though this weren't quite enough artistic achievement, there's puzzlework marquetry worthy of MC Escher in the **coro** (choir stalls), Bellini's achingly sweet *Madonna with Child* triptych in the **sacristy**, Paolo Veneziano's 1339 *Mother and Child with Worshipping Doge* – all eloquent hand gestures – in the **Sala del Capitolo**, and Bartolomeo Vivarini's *St Mark Enthroned* in the **Capella Corner**.

In the middle of the nave, the burden of Baldassare Longhena's **Doge Pesaro funereal monument** is carried by four huge black marble figures bursting from ragged clothes, powerful but undeniably suggestive of slavery. Bringing up the rear are disconsolate mourners dabbing at their eyes on Canova's **pyramid mausoleum**, originally intended as a monument to Titian. The great painter was lost to the plague at the age of 90 in 1576, but legend has it that, in light of his contributions here, Venice's strict rules of quarantine were bent to allow Titian's burial near his masterpiece.

★ Top Tips

- No food is allowed in the church and picture-taking is discouraged. Appropriate dress is also required (eg no shorts, miniskirts or midriff- or tank-tops).
- Download a brochure of the basilica or grab a map at the ticket desk for a DIY tour of the incredible range of artworks.
- An audio guide (€2) is available in six languages.
- Atmospheric concerts are occasionally held in the church. Check the website for the schedule.

Take a Break

Take a break to lunch beneath the grapevine at Trattoria da Ignazio (p108), or stroll a little further to cosy Vineria all'Amarone (p110) for hearty plates of gnocchi and a range of Veneto wines.

Top Experience

Find Fresh Food at Rialto Market

At this market they have known for 700 years that food tastes better when it's seasonal and local. Before there was a bridge at the Rialto or palaces along the Grand Canal, there was a Pescaria (fish market) and a produce market. So loyal are locals and Venice's restauranteurs to their market that talk of opening a larger, more convenient mainland fish market was swiftly crushed.

MAP P100, G3

Ponte di Rialto

A superb feat of engineering, Antonio da Ponte's 1591 Istrian stone span took three years and 250,000 gold ducats (about €19 million today) to construct. High arched, lined with shops and adorned with stone reliefs depicting St Mark, St Theodore and the Annunciation, the bridge crosses the Grand Canal at its narrowest point, connecting the neighbourhoods of San Polo and San Marco.

Pescaria

Slinging fresh fish for seven centuries and still going strong, the fishmongers of the Pescaria are more vital to Venetian cuisine than any chef. Starting at 7am, they sing the praises of today's catch: mountains of glistening *moscardini* (baby octopus), icebergs of inky *seppie* (cuttlefish) and buckets of crabs, from tiny *moeche* (soft-shell crabs) to *granseole* (spider crabs).

Sustainable fishing practices are not a new idea here; marble plaques show regulations set centuries ago for the minimum allowable sizes for lagoon fish. Nearly all the seafood is locally sourced, and much of it ends up on the plates of Venice's Michelin-starred restaurants.

Produce Market

Veneto *verdure* (vegetables) intrigue with their other-worldly forms, among them Sant'Erasmo *castraure* (baby artichokes), white Bassano asparagus and *radicchio di Treviso* (red, bitter chicory). In winter, look out for prized *rosa di Gorizia,* a rose-shaped chicory specimen, often eaten raw with honey, vinegar and pancetta in its native region Friuli Venezia Giulia.

★ Top Tips

- Tuesday and Friday are the best market days; the Pescaria is closed on Monday.
- The fish stalls are all packed up by 2pm, but a few stalls usually linger on into the afternoon, selling produce, nuts, dried fruit and cooking oils.
- Locally sourced fish and produce is labelled 'Nostrana'.
- Packaged herbs for making classic Italian dishes make a good gift.

Take a Break

Join thirsty shoppers at cubby-hole Al Mercà (p109) for a chilled glass of Franciacorta.

After they pack up their stalls in the Pescaria, most fishmongers head to All'Arco (p106).

Walking Tour

Venice Culinary Adventure

Before there were painters, opera divas or doges in Venice, there were fishmongers and grocers at the Rialto, bragging shamelessly about their wares. Today, the trade-route cuisine they inspired fills this corner of Venice with delectable discoveries for all your senses. Follow your growling stomach to find them on this culinary walking tour.

Walk Facts

Start Rialto Market; *vaporetto* Rialto Mercato

Finish Majer; *vaporetto* San Stae

Length 1.3km; 1.5 hours

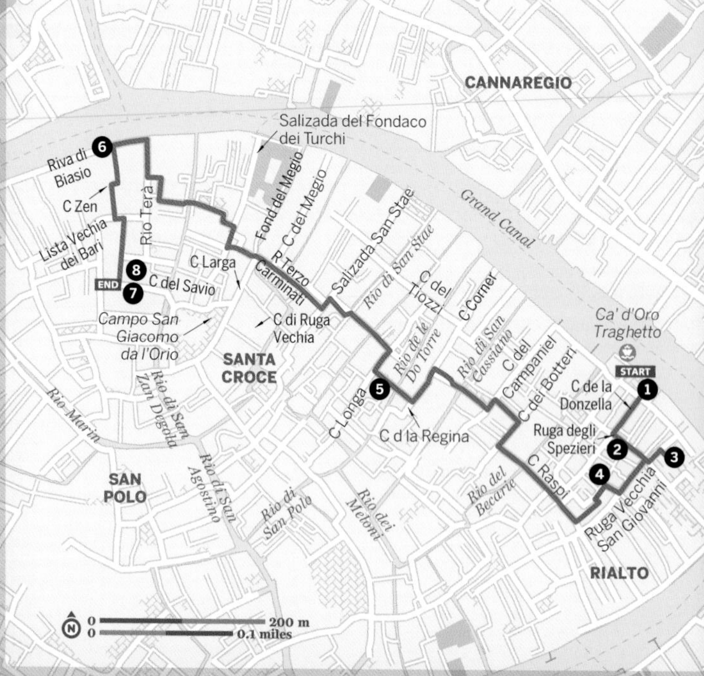

❶ Rialto Market

A trip through gourmet history starts at this **market** (p94), with its roofed Pescaria, where fishmongers artfully arrange the day's catch atop hillocks of ice.

❷ Drogheria Mascari

Glimpse trade-route treasures that made Venice's fortune at this **gourmet showcase** (www.imascari.com). Spice pyramids grace the windows, while specialty sweets are dispensed from copper-topped apothecary jars.

❸ Casa del Parmigiano

Displays of local San Daniele ham, Taleggio cheese and pepper-studded pecorinos at **Casa del Parmigiano** are reminders that Veneto's culinary fame wasn't built on seafood and spices alone.

❹ All'Arco

Duck into **All'Arco** (p106) for the city's best *cicheti* (Venetian tapas) – ask for *una fantasia* (a fantasy), and father-son chefs Francesco and Matteo will invent a dish with ingredients you just saw at the market.

❺ Veneziastampa

Cross a couple of bridges until you smell ink drying on letterpress menus and cookbook ex libris labels at **Veneziastampa** (p112).

❻ Riva di Biasio

Walk this sunny **Grand Canal footpath** allegedly named after 16th-century butcher Biagio (Biasio) Cargnio, whose sausages contained a special ingredient: children. When found out, Biasio was drawn and quartered.

❼ Gelato di Natura

Tradition meets innovation at this **gelato shop** (p108), which uses the finest DOP- and IGT-accredited local ingredients to make unusual small-batch flavours, along with vegan gelato and the East-meets-West *michi*, a Japanese rice cake with a gelato centre.

❽ Majer

Happy-hour temptations encircle Campo San Giacomo dell'Orio, but gourmet adventures deserve a glowing glass of natural-process wine at **Majer**.

Walking Tour

Fashion Finds in San Polo

Hunt for treasures at San Polo artisan studios and design boutiques, and find your own signature Venetian style to stand out in any opening-night crowd. From one-of-a-kind paper jewels to custom velvet slippers, the city's unique boutiques ensure no one can steal your look – and they usually cost less than global brands.

Walk Facts

Start Oh My Blue; *vaporetto* San Tomà

Finish Alberto Sarria; *vaporetto* San Stae

Length 1.4km; one hour

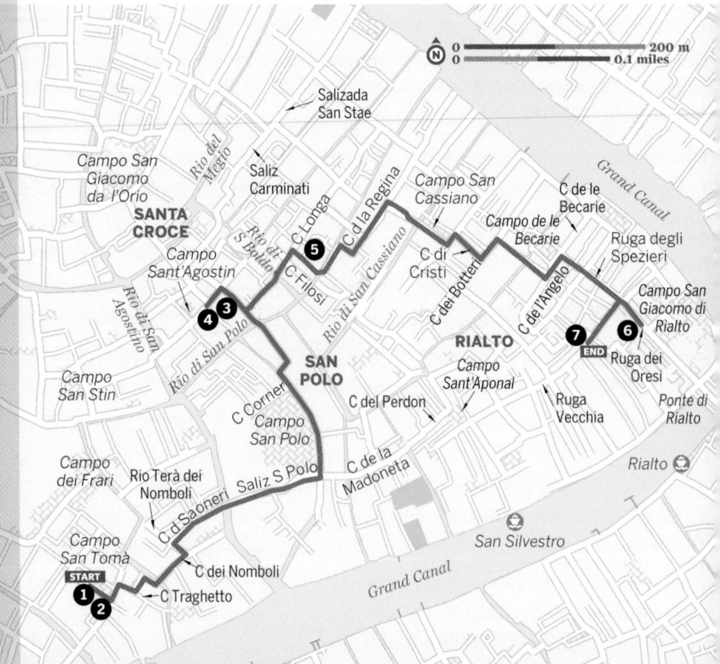

❶ Oh My Blue

Although **Oh My Blue** showcases the work of both international and local artists, owner Elena Rizzi's eye for colour, form and texture results in a jewellery collection that feels uniquely Venetian. Some iridescent silk clothes complement the contemporary art jewellery.

❷ La Bauta

Whether it's a unicorn or a steam-punk explorer mask you're after, traditional workshops at **La Bauta** will see you right. Alternatively, paint your own plague doctor or sun/moon look in an hour-long session, while learning about Venice's long-standing infatuation with playing dress up.

❸ Tabarro San Marco

There's a glorious jumble of Panama, straw and cotton hats here, but the real draw at **Tabarro San Marco** (www.tabarrosanmarco.com) are the dramatic woollen *tabarri*, the city's trademark cloak. They will set you back around €800, but you'll cut a fine dash on a winter's night.

❹ Spazio Manuzio

From orange resin swirls painted on the floor to Dorian Gray-esque portraits on the walls, **Spazio Manuzio** makes a gorgeous assault on the senses. Self-proclaimed as a 'gallery of emotion', it also features some dazzling one-off couture pieces: brocaded, screen-printed with growling tigers, asymmetrical and desirable. Check out the huge wooden loom where the scarves are created.

❺ Paperoowl

Stefania Giannici folds, prints, rolls, weaves and handpaints an extraordinary array of paper artworks at **Paperoowl**. Must-haves include delicate wind chimes inspired by Venetian domes and chic necklaces that look like Murano glass beads, but at a fraction of the price.

❻ Pied à Terre

Venetian slippers stay stylish with colourful *furlane* (slippers) at **Pied à Terre**. Handcrafted with recycled bicycle-tyre treads, they are ideal for finding your footing on a gondola. Choose from velvet, brocade or raw silk in vibrant shades of lemon, ruby and azure blue. Don't see your size? Shoes can be custom-made and shipped.

❼ Alberto Sarria

One of the few traditional mask-makers left in Venice, **Alberto Sarria** produces creations rendered in watercolour, acrylic and fine gilding, revealing the originality and subtle beauty of a master artisan. Aside from traditional masquerade and *commedia dell'arte* masks, Alberto also makes delightful marionettes, featuring figures such as Arlecchino and the Bauta Uomo, two notorious characters from Venetian theatre.

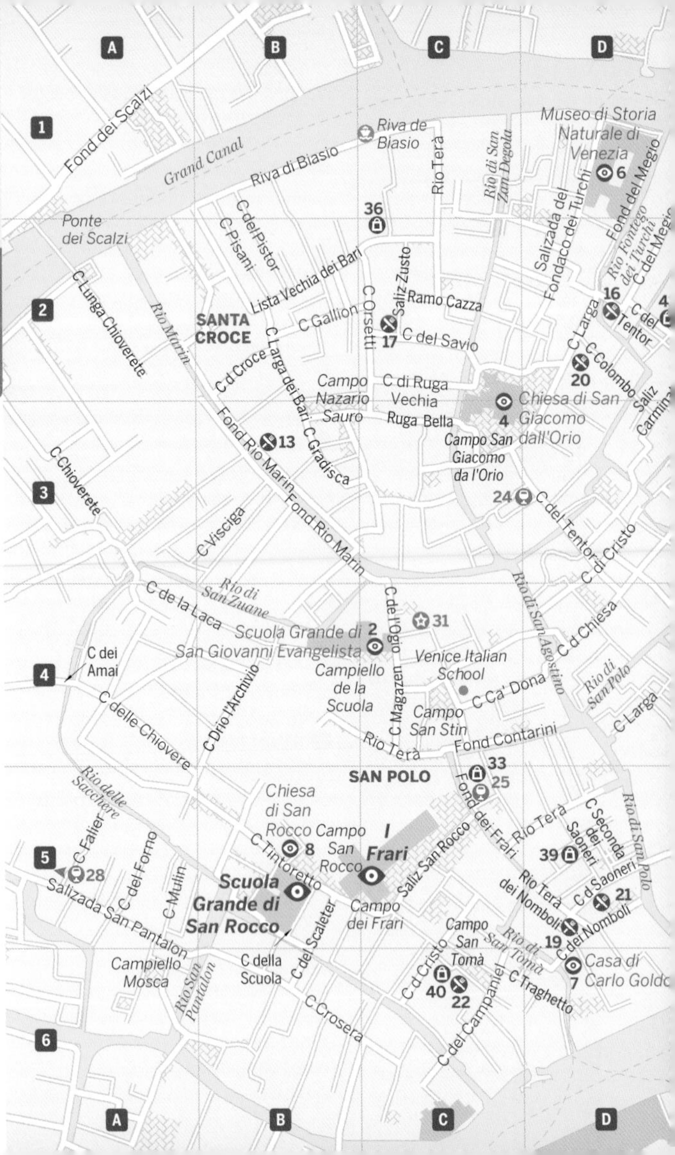

A B C D

1 2 3 4 5 6

Fond dei Scalzi
Grand Canal
Riva de Biasio
Riva di Biasio
Ponte dei Scalzi
Rio Terà
Rio di San Zan Degola
Museo di Storia Naturale di Venezia
6
Salizada del Fondaco dei Turchi
Fond del Megio
Rio Fontego dei Turchi
C del Megio
36
C del Pistor
C Pisani
Lista Vechia dei Bari
Saliz Zusto
Ramo Cazza
C Orsetti
C Gallion
SANTA CROCE
17
C del Savio
16
C del Tentor
4
C Larga
C Colombo
20
C Lunga Chioverete
Rio Marin
C d Croce
C Larga dei Bari
Campo Nazario Sauro
C di Ruga Vechia
Ruga Bella
Chiesa di San Giacomo dall'Orio
4
Campo San Giacomo da l'Orio
Saliz Carmini
Fond Rio Marin
13
C Gradisca
C Chioverete
24
C del Tentor
C di Cristo
C Visciga
Fond Rio Marin
Rio di San Zuane
C de la Laca
C del'Ogio
31
Rio di San Agostino
C d Chiesa
Scuola Grande di San Giovanni Evangelista
2
C dei Amai
Venice Italian School
Campiello de la Scuola
C Drio l'Archivio
C Magazen
C Ca' Dona
Rio di San Polo
Campo San Stin
C Larga
C delle Chiovere
Rio Terà
Fond Contarini
SAN POLO
33
25
Rio delle Sacchere
Chiesa di San Rocco
8
Campo San Rocco
I Frari
Fond dei Frari
Rio Terà
C Seconda dei Saoneri
Rio di San Polo
C Tintoretto
Saliz San Rocco
39
C Falier
28
C del Forno
C Mulin
Scuola Grande di San Rocco
Campo dei Frari
Rio Terà dei Nomboli
C d Saoneri
21
Salizada San Pantalon
C del Scaleter
Campo San Tomà
Rio di San Tomà
19
C dei Nomboli
Campiello Mosca
Rio San Pantalon
C della Scuola
C d Cristo
40
22
C Traghetto
Casa di Carlo Goldo
7
C Crosera
C del Campaniel

A B C D

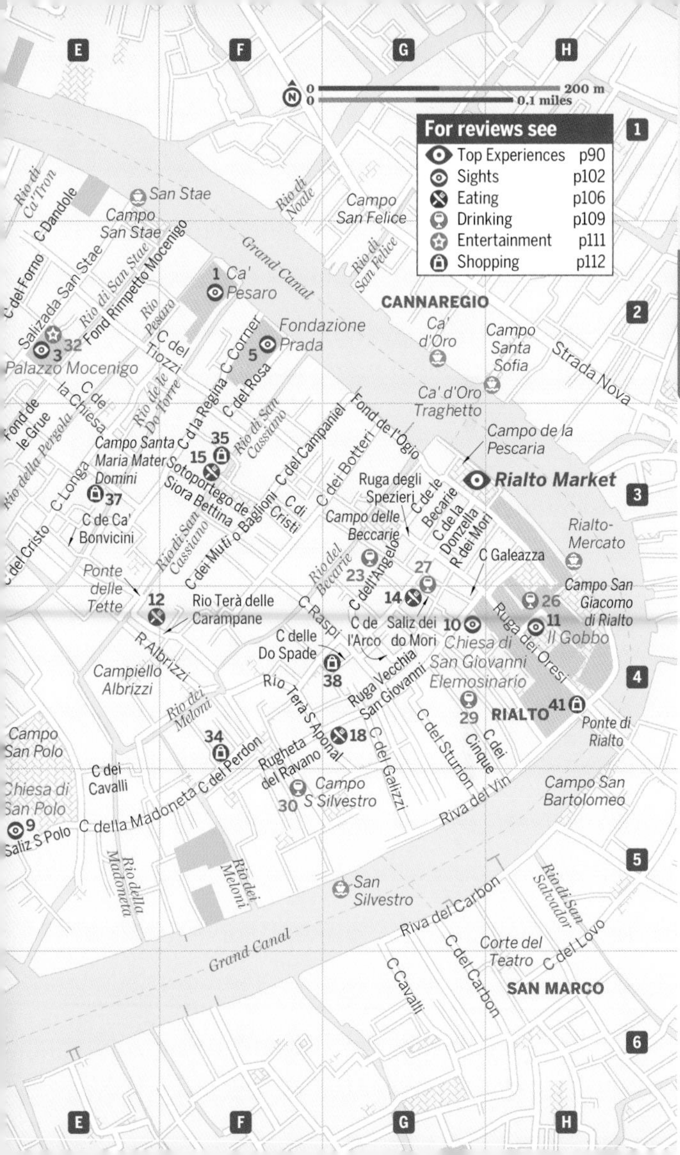

E
F
G
H
0 200 m
0 0.1 miles
For reviews see
Top Experiences p90
Sights p102
Eating p106
Drinking p109
Entertainment p111
Shopping p112
1
2
3
4
5
6
Rio di Ca' Tron
C Dandole
San Stae
Campo San Stae
C del Forno
Salizada San Stae
Rio di San Stae
Fond Rimpetto Mocenigo
Rio Pesaro
1 Ca' Pesaro
Grand Canal
Rio di Noale
Campo San Felice
Rio di San Felice
CANNAREGIO
Fondazione Prada
5
C Corner
C del Tiozzi
Rio de le Do Torre
3
32
Palazzo Mocenigo
C de la Chiesa
Fond de le Grue
Rio della Pergola
C d la Regina
C del Rosa
Rio di San Cassiano
Ca' d'Oro
Campo Santa Sofia
Strada Nova
Ca' d'Oro Traghetto
Fond de l'Ogio
C del Campaniel
C dei Botteri
Campo de la Pescaria
Rialto Market
35
15
Campo Santa Maria Mater Domini
Sotoportego de Siora Bettina
C Longa
37
C de Ca' Bonvicini
C del Cristo
Rio di San Cassiano
C dei Mufi o Baglioni
C di Cristi
Ruga degli Spezieri
Campo delle Beccarie
C de le Becarie
C de la Donzella
R dei Mori
Rialto-Mercato
C Galeazza
Ponte delle Tette
12
Rio Terà delle Carampane
Rio del Becarie
23
C dell'Angelo
27
14
Campo San Giacomo di Rialto
26
C Raspi
C de l'Arco
Saliz dei do Mori
10
Chiesa di San Giovanni Elemosinario
Ruga dei Oresi
11
Il Gobbo
R Albrizzi
C delle Do Spade
38
Campiello Albrizzi
Rio Terà S Aponal
Ruga Vecchia San Giovanni
29
RIALTO
41
Ponte di Rialto
Rio dei Meloni
34
Campo San Polo
Chiesa di San Polo
C dei Cavalli
C del Perdon
Rugheta del Ravano
18
C del Galizzi
C del Sturion
C dei Cinque
Campo S Silvestro
30
Riva del Vin
Campo San Bartolomeo
9
Saliz S Polo
C della Madoneta
Rio della Madoneta
Rio dei Meloni
San Silvestro
Riva del Carbon
Rio di San Salvador
Grand Canal
C del Carbon
Corte del Teatro
C del Lovo
C Cavalli
SAN MARCO
E
F
G
H

Sights

Ca' Pesaro

MUSEUM

1 MAP P100, F2

The stately exterior of this Baldassare Longhena–designed 1710 *palazzo* (mansion) hides two intriguing art museums that could hardly be more different: the **Galleria Internazionale d'Arte Moderna** and the **Museo d'Arte Orientale**. While the former includes art showcased at La Biennale di Venezia, the latter holds treasures from Prince Enrico di Borbone's epic 1887–89 souvenir-shopping spree across Asia. Competing with the artworks are Ca' Pesaro's fabulous painted ceilings, which reflect the power and prestige of the Pesaro clan. (www.capesaro.visitmuve.it)

Scuola Grande di San Giovanni Evangelista

HISTORIC BUILDING

2 MAP P100, C4

One of Venice's five main religious confraternities, the lay brothers of St John the Evangelist performed works of charity but also supported the arts by lavishing their clubrooms with treasures by the city's most famous painters and architects. Highlights include Pietro Lombardo's elaborately carved Renaissance **entry gate** (1481), topped with the eagle of St John; a Mauro Codussi-designed **staircase** (1498); and Giorgio Massari's spectacularly ostentatious **St John's Hall** (1727–62). (www.scuolasangiovanni.it)

Palazzo Mocenigo

MUSEUM

3 MAP P100, E2

Venice received a dazzling addition to its property portfolio in 1945 when Count Alvise Nicolò Mocenigo bequeathed his family's 17th-century *palazzo* to the city. While the ground floor hosts temporary exhibitions, the *piano nobile* (main floor) is where you'll find a dashing collection of historic fashion, including exquisitely embroidered men's silk waistcoats. Adding to the glamour and intrigue is an exhibition dedicated to the art of fragrance – an ode to Venice's 16th-century status as Europe's capital of perfume. (www.mocenigo.visitmuve.it)

Chiesa di San Giacomo dall'Orio

CHURCH

4 MAP P100, C3

Romanesque St James' Church was founded in the 9th century and completed in Latin-cross form in 1225; look up to see its handsome ship's keel ceiling. Within the serene gloom of the interior, notable artworks include a rare Lorenzo Lotto *Madonna with Child and Saints* (1546) and an exceptional Paolo Veneziano crucifix (c 1350), Christ's agony depicted with quiet grace. A green marble column, praised by Ruskin, was most likely brought here from Byzantium. (www.chorusvenezia.org)

Fondazione Prada

NOTABLE BUILDING

5 MAP P100, F2

This stately Grand Canal palace – designed by Domenico Rossi and completed in 1728 – has been commandeered by Fondazione Prada, which is renovating the palace. In between restoration work, frescoed Ca' Corner is the setting for slick temporary exhibitions of avant-garde art, notably during the Biennale. Otherwise, groups of six people or more can visit the palace free of charge between noon and 6pm on Friday. Bookings required a week in advance. (www.fondazioneprada.org)

Museo di Storia Naturale di Venezia

MUSEUM

6 MAP P100, D1

Never mind the doge: insatiable curiosity rules Venice, and inside the former Fondaco dei Turchi (the Turkish Trading House, rebuilt in the 1660s), it runs wild. The story begins upstairs with dinosaurs and prehistoric crocodiles, then dashes through evolution to Venice's age of colonial expansion, with a gallery devoted to the disturbingly violent forays of 19th-century adopted Venetian Giovanni Mani into Sudan. There's also a courtyard and attractive back garden, which is open during museum hours and ideal for picnics. (www.msn.visitmuve.it)

Chiesa di San Giacomo dall'Orio

Casa di Carlo Goldoni MUSEUM

7 MAP P100, D6

Venetian playwright Carlo Goldoni (1707–93) mastered second and third acts: he was a doctor's apprentice before switching to law, which proved handy when an *opera buffa* (comic opera) didn't sell. But as the 1st-floor display at his birthplace explains, Goldoni had the last laugh with his social satires. There's not really much to see here; the highlight is an 18th-century puppet theatre. (www.carlogoldoni.visitmuve.it)

Chiesa di San Rocco CHURCH

8 MAP P100, B5

Built by Bartolomeo Bon between 1489 and 1508 to house the remains of its titular saint, beautiful St Roch's Church received a baroque facelift between 1765 and 1771, which included a grand portal flanked by Giovanni Marchiori statues. Bon's rose window was moved to the side of the church, near the architect's original side door. On either side of the main altar are four vast paintings by Tintoretto depicting St Roch's life. The saint's casket is positioned above the altar. (www.scuolagrandesanrocco.org)

Chiesa di San Polo CHURCH

9 MAP P100, E5

Travellers pass St Paul's Church (founded in the 9th century) without guessing that major dramas unfold inside. Under the *carena di nave* (ship's keel) ceiling, Tintoretto's *Last Supper* (1569) on the rear wall shows apostles alarmed by Jesus'

Scuola Grande di San Rocco (left, p90) and Chiesa di San Rocco (right)

Venice in Quarantine

When the Black Death ravaged Europe, Venice mounted an interfaith effort against the plague. The city dedicated a church and *scuola* (religious confraternity) to San Rocco where Venetians could pray for deliverance from the disease, while also consulting resident Jewish and Muslim doctors about prevention measures. Venice established the world's first quarantine zone, with inspections and 40 (*quaranta*)-day waiting periods for incoming ships at Lazaretto. The city's forward-thinking, inclusive approach created Scuola Grande di San Rocco's artistic masterpieces, which provide comfort to the afflicted and bereaved to this day, and set a public-health standard that has saved countless lives down the centuries.

During the city's recent COVID-19 lockdown in 2020, social media exploded with images of swans and dolphins in the canals and nature in recovery. Some of the footage turned out to be fake, but a year later a mother and juvenile dolphin did swim up the Giudecca, to the joy of onlookers. And throughout the Venice lockdown, marine life was revealed in the unusually clear canal waters, without umpteen boats swirling sediment through them.

announcement that one of them will betray him. Giandomenico Tiepolo's *Way of the Cross* cycle in the Oratorio del Crocifisso (accessed from the rear of the church) shows onlookers tormenting an athletic Jesus, who leaps triumphantly from his tomb in the ceiling panel. (www.chorusvenezia.org)

Chiesa di San Giovanni Elemosinario — CHURCH

10 MAP P100, G4

Hunkering behind T-shirt kiosks is this soaring brick church, built by Scarpagnino after a disastrous fire in 1514 destroyed much of the Rialto area. Cross the threshold to witness flashes of Renaissance genius: Titian's tender *St John the Almsgiver* (1545) altarpiece and gloriously restored dome frescoes of frolicking angels by Pordenone. (www.chorusvenezia.org)

Il Gobbo — STATUE

11 MAP P100, H4

Rubbed for luck for centuries, this 1541 statue is now protected by an iron railing. *Il Gobbo* (The Hunchback) bends double to support stone steps, and served as a podium for official proclamations and punishments: those guilty of misdemeanours were forced to run a gauntlet of jeering citizens from Piazza San Marco to the Rialto. The minute they touched the statue their punishment was complete.

Eating

Antiche Carampane

VENETIAN €€€

12 MAP P100, E4

Hidden in the once shady lanes behind Ponte de le Tette, this culinary indulgence is hard to find but worth the effort. Once you do, say hello to a market-driven menu of Venetian classics, including *fegato alla Veneziana* (veal liver with onions) and lots of seafood. It's never short of a smart, convivial crowd, so it's a good idea to book ahead. (www.antichecarampane.com)

Osteria Trefanti

VENETIAN €€

13 MAP P100, B3

La Serenissima's spice trade lives on at simple, elegant Trefanti, where gnocchi might get an intriguing kick from cinnamon, and turbot is flavoured with almond and coconut. Seafood is the focus; try the 'doge's fettucine', with mussels, scampi and clams. Furnished with recycled copper lamps, the space is small and deservedly popular – so book ahead to sit inside or outside on the canal. (www.osteriatrefanti.it)

All'Arco

VENETIAN €

14 MAP P100, G4

Search out this authentic neighbourhood bar for some of the best *cicheti* in town. Armed with ingredients from the nearby Rialto Market, father-son team Francesco and Matteo serve miniature masterpieces to the scrum of eager patrons crowding the counter and spilling out onto the street. Even with copious prosecco, hardly any meal here tops €20.

Al Nono Risorto

ITALIAN €

15 MAP P100, F3

In the heart of Santa Croce, this bustling, bare-bones trattoria with its green shutters opening onto a vine- and lantern-hung terrace has an endearingly old-fashioned vibe. Service is mostly cheerfully efficient, and plates are heaped with squid-ink pasta, pizza and Venetian specials such as *sarde in saor* and *fegato alla Veneziana*. (https://alnonorisortovenezia.com)

Osteria La Zucca

ITALIAN €€

16 MAP P100, D2

With its menu of seasonal vegetarian creations and classic meat dishes, this cosy, wood-lined restaurant consistently hits the mark. Herbs and spices are used to great effect in dishes such as the nutmeg-tinged pumpkin and smoked ricotta flan. The small interior can get toasty, so reserve canalside seats in summer. Good gluten-free options. (www.lazucca.it)

Trattoria Antica Besseta

VENETIAN €€€

17 MAP P100, C2

Wood panelling sets the scene at this veteran 1887 trattoria, known for giving contemporary verve to regional classics such as *bigoli in salsa* (wholemeal pasta with anchovies and onions), *saor* (onion marinade), seafood dishes and tiramisu. The dapper owner is a trained sommelier, a fact reflected in the inspired wine list. (www.anticabesseta.it)

Ostaria dai Zemei — VENETIAN €

18 MAP P100, G4

Running this closet-sized *cicheti* counter are *zemei* (twins) Franco and Giovanni, who serve loyal regulars small bites with plenty of imagination: gorgonzola lavished with *peperoncino* (chilli) marmalade, duck breast drizzled with truffle oil, or chicory paired with leek and marinated anchovies. It's a gourmet bargain for inspired snacks and impeccable wines – try a crisp *nosiola* or invigorating prosecco brut. (www.ostariadaizemei.it)

Bar Ai Nomboli — SANDWICHES €

19  MAP P100, D5

This snappy place is never short of local professors, labourers and clued-in out-of-towners. Crusty rolls are packed with local cheeses, fresh greens, roast vegetables, salami, prosciutto and roast beef, and served at an antique marble lunch counter. Beyond standard mayo, condiments range from spicy mustard to wild-nettle sauce and fig salsa. Cheap, filling and scrumptious.

Trattoria Antica Besseta

Gelato di Natura

GELATO €

20 MAP P100, D2

Along with a dozen other things, Marco Polo is said to have introduced ice cream to Venice after his odyssey to China. At this gelato shop the experimentation continues with vegan versions of your favourite flavours, Japanese rice cakes and the creamiest, small-batch gelato incorporating accredited Italian ingredients such as Bronte pistachios, Piedmontese hazelnuts and Amalfi lemons. (www.gelatodinatura.com)

Trattoria da Ignazio

VENETIAN €€

21 MAP P100, D5

Dapper white-jacketed waiters serve pristine grilled lagoon fish, fresh pasta and desserts made in-house with a proud flourish, on tables bedecked with yellow linen. On cloudy days, homemade crab pasta with a bright Lugana white wine make a fine substitute for sunshine. On sunny days and warm nights, the neighbourhood converges beneath the garden's grape arbour. (www.trattoriadaignazio.com)

Basegò

VENETIAN €

22 MAP P100, C6

Focusing on three essential ingredients – good food, good wine and good music – this new-wave *cicheti* bar has rapidly formed a faithful following. Indulge in a feast of lagoon seafood, prosciutto, smoked tuna, salami and cheese heaped on small slices of fresh

Cicheti (p12)

ABIGAIL BLASI ©

bread. There's more seating than in most bars of this kind, and a dedicated kids' drawing area. (www.basego.it)

Drinking

Cantina Do Spade

WINE BAR

23 MAP P100, G3

Famously mentioned in Casanova's memoirs, cosy 'Two Spades' was founded in 1488 and continues to keep Venice in good spirits with its bargain Tri-Veneto and Istrian wines and young, laid-back management. Come early for market-fresh *fritture* (fried battered seafood) and grilled squid, or linger longer with satisfying, sit-down dishes such as *bigoli in salsa* (pasta in anchovy and onion sauce). (www.cantinadospade.com)

Osteria da Filo

BAR

24 MAP P100, D3

A citrus-painted living room where drinks are served, this locals' hang-out comes complete with piano, creaky sofas, free wi-fi, abandoned novels and the occasional live-music gig. Drinks are cheap and the Venetian tapas tasty. (www.facebook.com/osteriadafilo)

Il Mercante

COCKTAIL BAR

25 MAP P100, C5

An hour's changeover is all it takes for **Caffè dei Frari** , founded back in 1870, to transform itself into its night-time guise as Venice's best cocktail bar. If you can't find anything that takes your fancy on the adventurous themed cocktail list, the expert bar team will create something to suit your mood. In winter, snuggle on a velvet sofa upstairs. (www.ilmercantevenezia.com)

Talk, Eat, Live Italian

You see a rental sign on a palace door and you start daydreaming: morning banter with the greengrocer, lunch-time gossip at the local *bacaro* (bar), perhaps an evening *ti amo* at a canalside restaurant. There's no doubt that a grasp of Italian will enrich your experience of Venice and enhance your understanding of the city's culture. To brush up your language skills, head to **Venice Italian School** (Map p100, C4; www.veniceitalianschool.com) run by Venetians Diego and Lucia Cattaneo, who offer excellent, immersive courses for adults and children between the ages of five and 13 years old.

Al Mercà

WINE BAR

26 MAP P100, H4

Discerning drinkers throng to this cupboard-sized counter on a Rialto Market square to sip on top-notch prosecco and other wines by the glass. Edibles usually include meatballs and mini *panini*.

Grab Some Shade

The roots of Venetian bar culture date back at least to the 1700s, when Casanova was frequenting Cantina Do Mori. The word *'bacaro'* (bar) derives from the name of the Roman wine god Bacchus, and the term *'ombra'* (a glass of wine) has its own uniquely Venetian etymology. Whereas in most parts of Italy, *ombra* simply means 'shade' or 'shadow', its slang use in Venice dates back to the days when Venetian wine merchants set up shop in the shadow of the San Marco bell tower, moving their wares throughout the day to stay out of the sun. In this context, *prendere un'ombra* (grab some shade) came to mean 'grab a glass of wine', an affectionate colloquialism that survives to this day.

Cantina Do Mori — WINE BAR

27 MAP P100, G3

You'll feel like you've stepped into a Rembrandt painting at venerable 'Two Moors', a dark, rustic bar with roots in the 15th century. Under gleaming, ceiling-slung copper pots, nostalgists swill one of around 40 wines by the glass, or slurp prosecco from old-school champagne coupes. Peckish? Bar bites include pickled onions with anchovies, succulent *polpette* (meatballs) and slices of *pecorino* (sheep's milk cheese).

Bacareto da Lele — BAR

28 MAP P100, A5

Pocket-sized Da Lele is perpetually jammed with students and workers, stopping for a cheap, stand-up *ombra* (small glass of wine) on their way to and from the train station. Scan the blackboard for the day's wines and pair them with a little plate with salami, cheese and a roll. It closes for much of August.

Caffè del Doge — CAFE

29 MAP P100, G4

Sniff your way to the affable Doge, where dedicated drinkers slurp their way through the menu of speciality imported coffees, from Ethiopian to Guatemalan, all roasted on the premises. If you feel especially inspired, you can even pick up a stove-top coffee percolator. Pastries and viscous hot chocolate are on hand for those needing a sweet fix. (www.caffedeldoge.com)

Vineria all'Amarone — WINE BAR

30 MAP P100, F5

The warm wood-panelled interior and huge selection of Veneto wines by the glass are just part of the popularity of this friendly bar-restaurant. Other reasons to stop by are generous *cicheti* platters, belly-warming plates of gnocchi and braised beef in red wine, and wine-tasting flights, which include the heady Amarone from which the bar takes its name. (www.allamarone.com)

Entertainment

Palazetto Bru Zane — CLASSICAL MUSIC

31 ★ MAP P100, C4

Pleasure palaces don't get more romantic than this little *palazzo* on concert nights, when exquisite harmonies tickle Sebastiano Ricci angels tumbling across stucco-frosted ceilings. Multi-year restorations returned 17th-century Casino Zane's 100-seat music room to its original function, attracting world-class musicians to enjoy its acoustics. Free guided tours of the building run on Thursdays (in Italian/French/English at 2.30pm/3pm/3.30pm; none in August). (www.bru-zane.com)

La Casa Del Cinema — CINEMA

32 ★ MAP P100, E2

Venice's public film archive shows original-language art films, including some in English, to members in a modern 50-seat, wood-beamed screening room inside Palazzo Mocenigo (p102). Check online for pre-release previews and revivals with introductions by directors, actors and scholars. (www.comune.venezia.it)

Al Mercà (p109)

Shopping

Process Collettivo

GIFTS & SOUVENIRS

33 MAP P100, C5

A nonprofit cooperative runs this little shop, selling Made in Prison goods made by inmates of Venice's jails as part of a social reintegration program. The toiletries are made from plants grown in the garden of the women's prison on Giudecca, while the very hip satchels and shoulder bags constructed from recycled advertising hoardings are made at the men's prison in Santa Croce. (www.rioteradeipensieri.org)

Damocle Edizioni

BOOKS

34 MAP P100, F4

A meeting point for writers, artists and readers, Damocle Edizioni is both a bijou bookshop and a publishing house, where Pierpaolo Pregnolato produces exquisite multilingual books and prints, including an Ai Weiwei limited-edition print in homage to Julian Assange. Emerging authors, out-of-print classics and rare unpublished works are his stock in trade, the handmade, hand-stitched books illustrated with original watercolours, woodcuts and even mosaic tesserae. (www.edizionidamocle.com)

Artigianato d'Arte di Mauro Vianello

GLASS

35 MAP P100, F3

A coral reef's worth of painstakingly detailed glass Nemos, seahorses, starfish, jellyfish and seashells fills the window of this little glass studio. Alternatively you could opt for a biologically accurate reproduction of a delicate butterfly or a glistening snail. Book a demonstration if you want to watch the artist at work. (www.maurovianello.com)

DoppioFondo

ARTS & CRAFTS

36 MAP P100, C2

Tiziano and Vanessa use a variety of printmaking techniques including silk screen and xylograph to create handmade T-shirts and tote bags, some with dreamy Venetian scenes. They are also independent publishers, producing charming limited-edition art books. The store hosts regular workshops and courses in activities including printmaking, calligraphy and drawing (in English and Italian). (www.doppiofondo.org)

Veneziastampa

ARTS & CRAFTS

37 MAP P100, E3

Mornings are best to catch the 1930s Heidelberg machine in action, but whenever you arrive, you'll find mementos hot off the in-house press. Veneziastampa recalls more elegant times, when postcards were gorgeously lithographed: your missives home will look much more impressive if you buy them here. And pick your signature symbols – meteors, faucets, trapeze artists – for original bookplates and cards. (www.veneziastampa.com)

Venice's 'Honest Courtesans'

The Age of Decadence

With trade revenues and the value of the Venetian ducat slipping in the 16th century, Venice's fleshpots brought in far too much valuable foreign currency to be outlawed. Instead, Venice opted for regulation and taxation. Rather than baring all in the rough-and-ready streets around the Rialto, prostitutes could only display their wares from the waist up in windows, or sit bare-legged on window sills. Venice decreed that to distinguish themselves from noblewomen who increasingly dressed like them, ladies of the night should ride in gondolas with red lights. By the end of the 16th century, the town was flush with some 12,000 registered prostitutes, creating a literal red-light district.

Education Pays

Venice's *cortigiane oneste* or 'honest courtesans' earned the title not by offering a fair price, but by providing added value with style and wit that reflected well on their patrons. They were not always beautiful or young, but *cortigiane oneste* were well educated, dazzling their admirers with poetry, music and apt social critiques. In the 16th century, some Venetian families spared no expense on their daughters' educations: beyond an advantageous marriage, educated women who became *cortigiane oneste* could command prices 60 times those of a *cortigiana di lume* ('courtesan of the lamp' – streetwalker).

An Alternative Guidebook

A catalogue of 210 of Venice's *piu honorate cortigiane* (most honoured courtesans) was published in 1565, listing contact information and rates, payable directly to the courtesan's servant, her mother or, occasionally, her husband. A *cortigiana onesta* might circulate in Venetian society as the known mistress of one or more admirers, who compensated her for her company rather than services rendered. Syphilis was an occupational hazard, and special hospices were founded for infirm courtesans.

Gmeiner

SHOES

38 MAP P100, G4

Gabriele Gmeiner honed her shoemaking craft at Hermès and John Lobb, and today jet-setters fly to Venice just for her ultra-sleek Oxfords with hidden 'bent' seams and her minutely hand-stitched brogues, made to measure for men and women (around €3000, including a hand-carved wooden last). There's no sign, but peek through the windows and you'll see Gabriele's shoemaking paraphernalia. (www.gabrielegmeiner.com)

Gilberto Penzo ARTS & CRAFTS

39 MAP P100, D5

Yes, you actually can take a gondola home in your pocket. Anyone fascinated by the models at the Museo Storico Navale (p143) will go wild here, amid handmade wooden models of Venetian boats, including some that are seaworthy (or at least bathtub worthy). Signor Penzo also creates kits, so crafty types and kids can have a crack at making one themselves. (www.veniceboats.com)

Il Baule Blu VINTAGE

40 MAP P100, C6

'The Blue Trunk' is a curiosity cabinet of elusive treasures where you can expect to stumble across anything from 1970s bubble sunglasses and antique Murano *murrine* (glass beads) to vintage Italian coats and frocks in good condition.

Emilio Ceccato CLOTHING

41 MAP P100, H4

If you've been eyeing up the natty striped T-shirts, devilishly soft winter wool hats and crepe pants sported by Venice's gondoliers then make a beeline for official supplier Emilio Ceccato. Here you'll find a huge selection of shirts, pants, jackets and water-

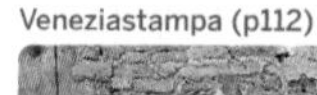

Veneziastampa (p112)

Top Four Venice Reads

The Aspern Papers A professor, obsessed with a long-dead poet, finds out he had an affair with a Venetian and tries to lay hands on a set of letters between the two. Henry James wrote this masterful novel in Venice in 1888.

Mona Erotic, ridiculous and clever, this little volume of poetry exemplifies the wit of Giorgio Baffo, Casanova's mentor. Venetians still love this book, which says a lot.

Venice Elegy Written in Chinese by poet Yang Lian, this elegy becomes trilingual with the beautiful translations in English and Italian.

Watermark Read Iosif Aleksandrovič Brodskij's novel to find a Venice of fog and dim lights, empty and spectral – like walking down Fondamenta degli Incurabili on a November afternoon.

Recommended by Pierpaolo Pregnolato,
publisher at Damocle Edizioni

proof shoulder bags, all emblazoned with the gondoliers' supercool logo. What's more, proceeds from purchases are reinvested in training programs and boatyards. (www.emilioceccato.com)

Bottega Orafa ABC JEWELLERY

42 MAP P100, D2

Master of metals Andrea d'Agostino takes his influence from the Japanese technique of *mokume gane* (meaning 'metal with woodgrain'), masterful examples of which are on display in the Asian gallery of Ca' Pesaro (p102). The result is rings, pendants and bracelets with swirling multicoloured patterns that seem to capture the dappled lagoon waters for all time in silver and gold. (www.orafaabc.com)

Explore Cannaregio & the Ghetto

While busy Strada Nova, parallel to the Grand Canal, bustles with tourists, wander a little deeper into Cannaregio and you will see the area turn residential, its canals crisscrossed with washing lines. Locals throng the buzzy canalside stretch of Fondamenta dei Ormesini for its cicheti *(Venetian tapas) bars and neighbourhood restaurants. Within the district is the once restricted area of the Ghetto, a living monument to the outsized contributions of Venice's Jewish community.*

The Short List

- ***The Ghetto (p118)*** *Exploring the historic precinct of Venice's centuries-old Jewish community.*
- ***Chiesa della Madonna dell'Orto (p124)*** *Paying homage to Tintoretto at his local church and burial place.*
- ***Galleria Giorgio Franchetti alla Ca' d'Oro (p124)*** *Finding Grand Canal photo ops and misappropriated masterpieces at this glorious Gothic* palazzo *(mansion).*

Getting There & Around

Vaporetto You can explore Cannaregio from three different stops on the Grand Canal: Ferrovia, San Marcuola and Ca' d'Oro, all of which are served by lines 1 and 2. From Ferrovia, take lines 4.1, 4.2, 5.1 and 5.2 to Fondamente Nove. Line 3 goes to Murano. From Fondamente Nove, lines 12 and 13 head to the northern islands.

Cannaregio & the Ghetto Map on p122

Canal in Cannaregio MARTON VARHOMOKI/SHUTTERSTOCK ©

Top Experience

Explore Campo del Ghetto Nuovo & the Ghetto

MAP P122, D3

This corner of Cannaregio once housed a getto (foundry), but its role as Venice's Jewish quarter from the 16th to 19th centuries gave the word new meaning. In the 12th century, there were more than 1300 Jews living in Venice, in Giudecca and Mestre. From 1516 onwards, the Jewish community was restricted to the gated island of Ghetto Nuovo (New Foundry), and the first 'Ghetto'.

Ghetto Tours

At the Ghetto's heart, the **Museo Ebraico** (Jewish Museum; www.museoebraico.it) explores the history of Venice's Jewish community through everyday artefacts. The museum is currently closed for restoration, but it continues to run its popular tours of the local synagogues.

The Synagogues

As you enter **Campo del Ghetto Nuovo**, look up and around you to spot the hidden synagogues through subtle indications.

Recognisable by its five long windows, the **Schola Tedesca** (German Synagogue) has been the spiritual home of Venice's Ashkenazi community since 1528. Inside, the baroque pulpit and carved benches are topped by a gilded, elliptical women's gallery, modelled after a Venetian opera balcony.

Squashed into the corner of the *campo* (square) is the wooden cupola of the **Schola Canton** (Corner Synagogue), built c 1531. Its gilded rococo interiors were added in the 18th century.

Over the bridge in **Campo del Ghetto Vecchio**, Sephardic Jewish refugees raised two synagogues that were later rebuilt in grander style, with 17th-century interiors. **Schola Levantina** (Levantine Synagogue) has a magnificent woodworked pulpit and a *yeshiva* (school room), while the **Schola Spagnola** (Spanish Synagogue) has exuberant marble and wooden baroque interiors.

★ Top Tips

- To explore the buildings inside the Ghetto, take one of the synagogue tours offered in English by the Museo Ebraico, departing hourly from 11am. Which synagogue you get to see depends on which day you take the tour.
- For information about local Jewish life, visit the **Jewish Community Info Point** (www.jvenice.org).

Take a Break

Ghetto Vecchio is home to one of Venice's best bakeries, Panificio Volpe Giovanni (p129), which serves a variety of baked Jewish goods.

Indulge in a tasty home-cooked lunch at family-run **Trattoria Pontini**.

Walking Tour

Cannaregio's Cicheti Circuit

You can dine and see the best of the district by grazing cicheti, *usually accompanied by an* ombra *(half-glass) of white wine. Platters appear on counters across Cannaregio at 6pm, from perfect* polpette *(meatballs) to top-notch* crudi *(Venetian-style sashimi laced with olive oil and/or aged balsamic vinegar). For bargain gourmet adventures, graze these Cannaregio cicheti hotspots.*

Walk Facts

Start Al Parlamento; *vaporetto* Crea

Finish Un Mondo Divino; *vaporetto* Rialto

Length 2km; one hour

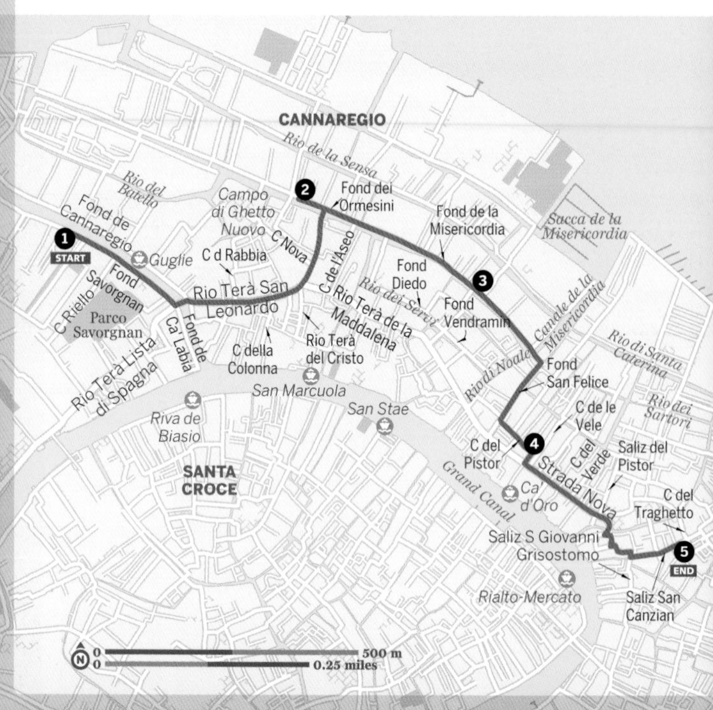

❶ Al Parlamento

Relaxed, welcoming **Al Parlamento** is a perennially popular haunt for a *spritz* (prosecco cocktail) accompanied by excellent overstuffed *tramezzini* (triangular stacked sandwiches), with great canal-bank views. There's occasional live music or DJs in the evenings.

❷ Al Timon

Sit with your feet dangling over the edge of the canal at **Timon** (www.altimon.it) and watch the parade of local drinkers and dreamers arrive for seafood crostini paired with a selection of organic and Denominazione d'Origine Controllata (DOC) wines by the *ombra* or carafe. Inside is wood-lined and cosy for the winter months.

❸ Vino Vero

Pint-sized **Vino Vero** (www.facebook.com/vinoverovenezia) is a glorious place, its walls lined with bottles of small-production, natural and biodynamic labels. The wine is combined with the cut-above *cicheti*, which arguably boasts the most mouth-watering display of continually replenished, fresh crostini in the entire city. There are outside canal-bank tables, but if you don't win one of those, you'll have to balance your snacks on the outdoor banquette.

❹ Ca' D'Oro alla Vedova

Tucked into a narrow *calle* (street) is **Ca' D'Oro alla Vedova**, or the 'Widow's House of Gold', Venice's oldest and most famous *osterie* (casual tavern), where you can snaffle its famous crispy meatballs, its superior and seasonal *cicheti* and its *ombre* at the bar with the local crowd. You can also choose to nab a table and dine on classic Venetian dishes, such as *bigoli in salsa* (thick wholemeal pasta with anchovies).

❺ Un Mondo Divino

Choose from delectable piles of snacks, such as marinated artichokes and *sarde in saor* (sardines in a tangy onion marinade), and claim a few square inches of ledge for your plate and glass. **Un Mondo Divino** offers plenty of wines by the glass, so take a chance on a unique blend or obscure varietal.

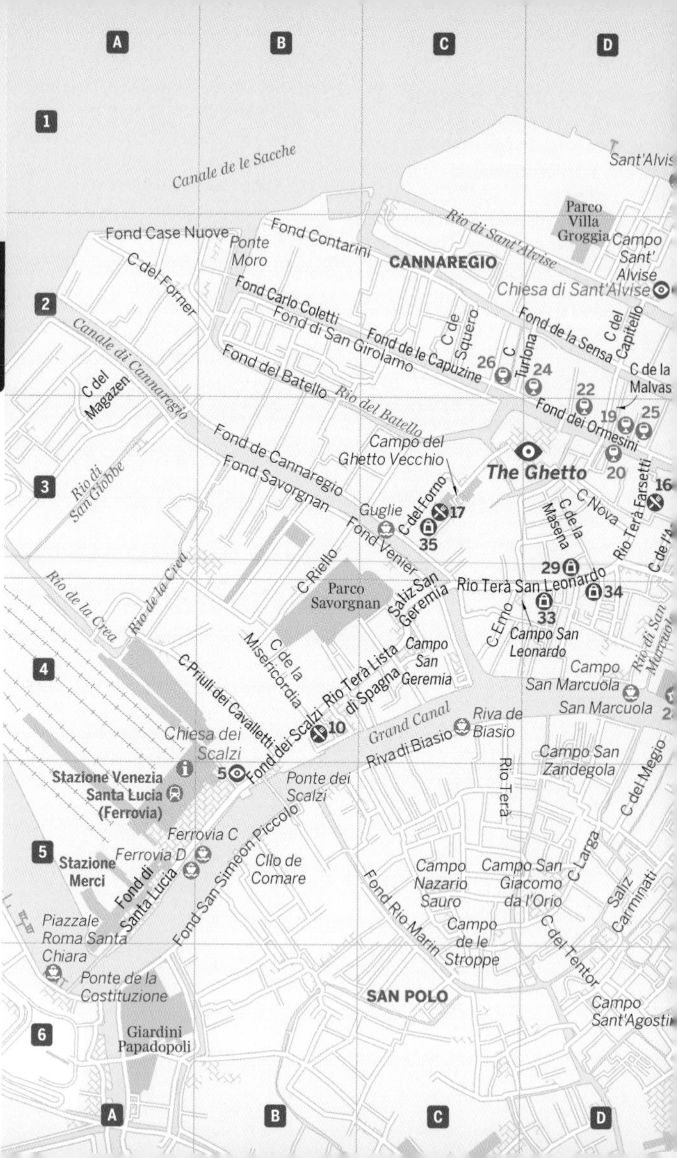

A
B
C
D
1
2
3
4
5
6
Canale de le Sacche
Sant'Alvis
Parco Villa Groggia
Campo Sant' Alvise
Chiesa di Sant'Alvise
Rio di Sant'Alvise
CANNAREGIO
Fond Case Nuove
Ponte Moro
Fond Contarini
C del Forner
Fond Carlo Coletti
Fond di San Girolamo
Fond de le Capuzine
C de Squero
C Turlona
26
24
Fond de la Sensa
C del Capitello
C de la Malvas
22
19
25
20
Fond dei Ormesini
Canale di Cannaregio
C del Magazen
Fond del Batello
Rio del Batello
Campo del Ghetto Vecchio
The Ghetto
Fond de Cannaregio
Fond Savorgnan
Rio di San Giobbe
Guglie
C del Forno
17
35
C Nova
C de la Masena
Rio Terà Farsetti
16
29
Fond Venier
C Riello
Parco Savorgnan
Rio de la Crea
Saliz San Geremia
Rio Terà San Leonardo
34
33
C Emo
Campo San Leonardo
Campo San Marcuola
San Marcuola
Rio di San Marcuola
C de la Misericordia
C Priuli dei Cavalletti
Rio Terà Lista di Spagna
Campo San Geremia
Grand Canal
Riva de Biasio
Riva di Biasio
10
Chiesa dei Scalzi
Fond dei Scalzi
Stazione Venezia Santa Lucia (Ferrovia)
5
Ponte dei Scalzi
Rio Terà
Campo San Zandegola
C del Megio
Ferrovia C
Ferrovia D
Stazione Merci
Fond di Santa Lucia
Fond San Simeon Piccolo
Cllo de Comare
Fond Rio Marin
Campo Nazario Sauro
Campo San Giacomo da l'Orio
C Larga
Saliz Carminati
Piazzale Roma Santa Chiara
Campo de le Stroppe
C del Tentor
Ponte de la Costituzione
SAN POLO
Campo Sant'Agosti
Giardini Papadopoli

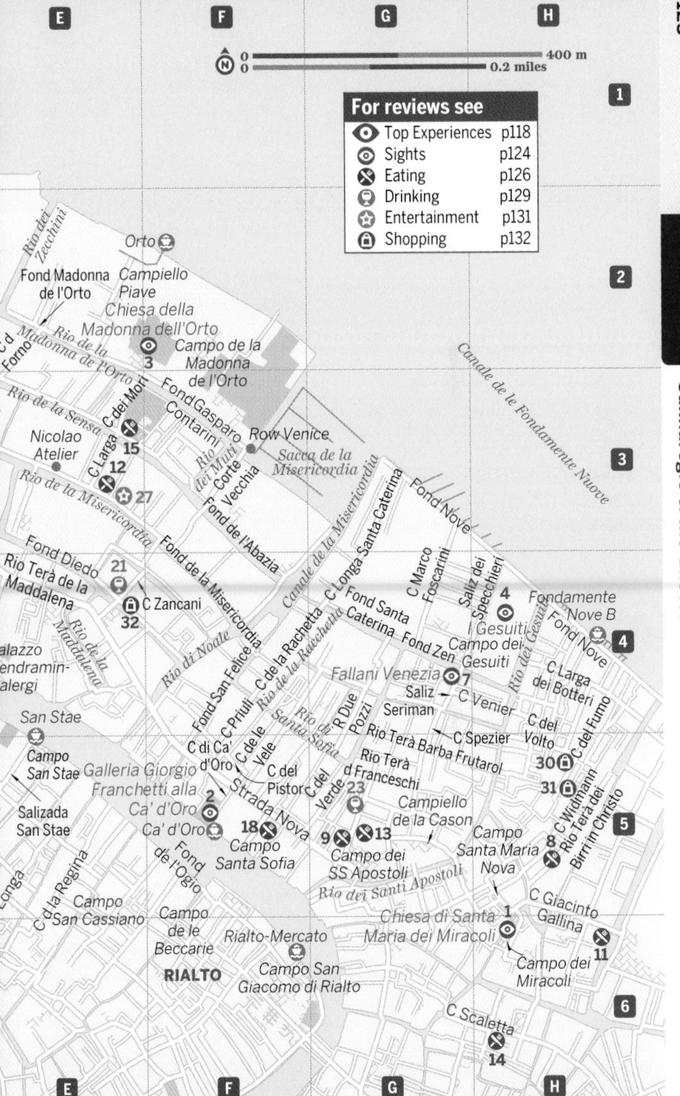
E
F
G
H
0 400 m
0 0.2 miles
1
2
3
4
5
6
For reviews see
Top Experiences p118
Sights p124
Eating p126
Drinking p129
Entertainment p131
Shopping p132
Rio dei Zecchini
Orto
Fond Madonna de l'Orto
Campiello Piave
Chiesa della Madonna dell'Orto
3
Campo de la Madonna de l'Orto
C d Forno
Rio de la Madonna de l'Orto
Rio de la Sensa
C dei Mori
Fond Gasparo Contarini
Row Venice
Sacca de la Misericordia
Canale de le Fondamente Nuove
Nicolao Atelier
15
C Larga
12
27
Rio dei Muti
Corte Vecchia
Rio de la Misericordia
Fond de l'Abazia
Canale de la Misericordia
C Longa Santa Caterina
Fond Nove
Fond Diedo
21
Rio Terà de la Maddalena
C Zancani
32
Fond de la Misericordia
C Marco Foscarini
Saliz dei Specchieri
4
Fondamente Nove B
Fond Nove
Rio de la Maddalena
Rio di Noale
C de la Rachetta
Rio de la Racchetta
Fond Santa Caterina
Fond Zen
I Gesuiti
Campo dei Gesuiti
Rio dei Gesuiti
Palazzo Vendramin-Calergi
Fond San Felice
C Priuli
Fallani Venezia
7
Saliz Seriman
C Venier
C Larga dei Botteri
San Stae
Rio di Santa Sofia
R Due Pozzi
Rio Terà Barba Frutarol
C Spezier
C del Volto
C del Fumo
Campo San Stae
C di Ca' d'Oro
C de le Vele
C del Pistor
C del Verde
Rio Terà d Franceschi
30
31
Galleria Giorgio Franchetti alla Ca' d'Oro
2
Strada Nova
23
Campiello de la Cason
C Widmann
Rio Terà dei Birri in Christo
Salizada San Stae
Ca' d'Oro
18
9
13
Campo Santa Sofia
Campo dei SS Apostoli
Campo Santa Maria Nova
8
Fond de l'Ogio
Rio dei Santi Apostoli
C la Regina
Campo San Cassiano
Campo de le Beccarie
Rialto-Mercato
Chiesa di Santa Maria dei Miracoli
1
C Giacinto Gallina
11
Campo dei Miracoli
RIALTO
Campo San Giacomo di Rialto
C Scaletta
14

Sights

Chiesa di Santa Maria dei Miracoli CHURCH

1 MAP P122, H6

This magnificent church was built in the 1480s to house Nicolò di Pietro's Madonna icon after the painting miraculously began weeping in its outdoor shrine. Pietro and Tullio Lombardo's design of the church used marble scavenged from slag heaps in San Marco and favoured the human scale of radically new Renaissance architecture in place of the grandiose Gothic status quo.

Galleria Giorgio Franchetti alla Ca' d'Oro MUSEUM

2 MAP P122, F5

Such was the splendour of the 15th-century Ca' d'Oro, with its lacelike Gothic loggias made by Lombardi artisans, that it was named the 'Golden House'. Baron Franchetti (1865–1922) restored and bequeathed this treasure-box palace to Venice, packed with his collection of masterpieces, many of which were originally plundered from Veneto churches during Napoleon's conquest of Italy. The baron himself designed the glorious mosaic of the open-sided courtyard. Treasures from the baron's collection include an arrow-riddled St Sebastian by Mantegna. (www.cadoro.org)

Venetian Mask-Making

Ca' Macana Atelier (p132) offers Venetian Carnevale mask-making workshops, from a basic one-hour mask-painting session that's ideal for kids (age three and up) to more involved papier-mâché instruction. Book ahead online.

Chiesa della Madonna dell'Orto CHURCH

3 MAP P122, F2

Named after a Madonna statue discovered in a nearby *orto* (orchard) and thought to perform miracles, this elegantly spare Gothic church from 1365 was also the parish church of Renaissance painter Tintoretto (1518–94), who is buried in the chapel to the right of the altar. Inside, you'll find two of Tintoretto's finest works: *Presentation of the Virgin in the Temple* and *Last Judgement*, where lost souls attempt to hold back a teal tidal wave while an angel rescues one last person from the ultimate *acqua alta* (high tide).

I Gesuiti CHURCH

4 MAP P122, H4

Giddily over the top, even by rococo standards, this glitzy 18th-century Jesuit church is difficult to take in all at once, with staggering white-and-green *intarsia* (inlaid marble) walls that resemble a Venetian form of flock wallpaper, marble curtains draped over the pulpit and a marble carpet spilling down the altar steps. While the ceiling is a riot of gold-and-white stuccowork, gravity is provided by Titian's uncharacteristically gloomy *Martyrdom of St Lawrence*, on the left as you enter the church.

Chiesa dei Scalzi CHURCH

5 MAP P122, B5

The Scalzi was a strict offshoot of the Carmelite order, and donors competed to fund the most opulent part of this church. It is Longhena-designed (built 1654–80), with a ripplingly ornate facade by Giuseppe Sardi – an unusual departure for Venice, where baroque ebullience was usually reserved for interiors. It was a deliberate echo of a Roman style to help make the Discalced (meaning 'barefoot'; *scalzi* in Italian) Carmelites posted here from Rome feel more at home. There's even an *Ecstacy of St Theresa* echoing Bernini's Roman masterpiece. (www.carmeloveneto.it)

Chiesa di Sant'Alvise CHURCH

6 MAP P122, D2

Don't be fooled by the bare brick exterior of this 1388 church, attached to an Augustinian convent. Inside, it's a riot of colour, with extraordinary *trompe l'œil* ceiling frescoes and massive canvases all around. Look out for Tiepolo's *La salita al Calvario* (The Road to Calvary), a distressingly human depiction of one of Christ's falls under the weight of the cross.

Fallani Venezia ARTS & CRAFTS

7 MAP P122, G4

Fiorenzo Fallani's laboratory has been credited with transforming

I Gesuiti

screenprinting from a medium of reproduction to an innovative and creative artistic technique. Check the website to sign up for workshops that will teach you the basics of screenprinting through to more complex processes, using a range of different colours, acetates and frames. Workshops can be booked for both individuals and families. This is also is a great place to purchase original art prints of Venice. (www.fallanivenezia.com)

Eating

Osteria Boccadoro VENETIAN €€€

The sweetly singing birds in this *campo* are probably angling for your leftovers, but they don't stand a chance. Chef-owner Luciano and son Simone's creative *crudi* are two-bite delights, and cloud-like gnocchi and homemade pasta are gone too soon. Fish is sourced from the lagoon or the Adriatic, and vegetables come from the restaurant's kitchen garden. (www.boccadorovenezia.it)

Ai Promessi Sposi VENETIAN €€

9 MAP P122, G5

Bantering Venetians thronging the bar are the only permanent fixtures at this wood-beamed neighbourhood *osteria* hidden in a street overlooked by Gothic windows. The ever-changing menu feature fresh Venetian seafood and Veneto meats at excellent prices. Seasonal standouts include *sarde in saor*

Preserving Venice

Venice is a microcosm of some of the biggest current global challenges, like environmental decadence, rising sea levels and erosion of social fabric by mass tourism. Local activist groups, like We Are Here Venice, are working to make Venice a better city.

- Consider making a donation to We Are Here Venice or helping to spread their message as part of your trip.
- Visit off-season. Venice is beautiful throughout the year, and overcrowding during the main holidays makes life difficult for Venetians.
- Venice is a lagoon. Try to spend at least a day getting to know this extraordinary habitat: learn about its dynamics and challenges, and explore the islands to enhance your understanding of Venetian civilisation by experiencing the relationship between city and nature.

Recommended by Jane da Mosto, *author of* We Are Here Venice, *@weareherevenice*

and *seppie in umido con polenta* (cuttlefish in rich tomato sauce with polenta), but pace yourself for heavenly tiramisu and excellent *semifreddo* (semi-frozen desserts).

Pasticceria Dal Mas BAKERY €

10 MAP P122, B4

This historic, stand-up Venetian bakery and cafe is lined with mirrors, marble and metal trim, fitting for the pastries displayed within. Despite the perpetual morning crush, the efficient team dispenses top-notch coffee and *cornetti* (Italian-style croissants) with admirable equanimity. The pistachio-flavoured *cornetti* are particularly delicious. Come mid-morning for mouthwatering, still-warm quiches. The hot chocolate is also exceptional. (There's a sibling chocolate shop next door.) (www.dalmaspasticceria.it)

Gelataria Ducale ICE CREAM €

11 MAP P122, H6

This unassuming place serves up some of Venice's finest ice cream. Peach that tastes of only the most fragrant varieties, lemon with substance, chocolate laced with ginger and their delectably creamy *crema ducale*. The flavours are limited but, come on, this is quality fit for a duke.

Osteria da Rioba VENETIAN €€€

12 MAP P122, E3

Taking the lead with fresh seafood and herbs pulled from the family's Sant'Erasmo farm, Da Rioba's creative kitchen turns out Venetian cuisine, but with an emphasis on the presentation as well as the taste. This is prime date-night territory. In winter, cosy up in the wood-beamed interior; in summer, sit canalside. Reservations recommended. (www.darioba.com)

Painting Venice

Sign up for a **Painting Venice** (www.paintingvenice.com) session with professionally trained and practising artists Caroline, Sebastien and Katrin, and you'll strike out into tranquil *campi* (squares) in the tradition of classic Venetian *vedutisti* (outdoor artists). It's a great way to slow down and really appreciate the colour and composition of each city view.

Trattoria da Bepi Già '54' VENETIAN €€

13 MAP P122, G5

Popular da Bepi is a traditional trattoria in the very best sense. The interior is a warm, wood-panelled cocoon and there are some streetside tables outside. Take their friendly advice on the classic Venetian menu and order sweet, steamed spider crab, briny razor clams, grilled turbot with artichokes and a tiramisu that doesn't disappoint. (www.dabepi.it)

Venetian Jewish History

Renaissance in the Ghetto

In the 14th century, pragmatic Venice granted Jewish communities the right to practise professions key to the city's livelihood, including medicine, trade, banking, fashion and publishing, if they paid a fee every five years. Despite a 10-year censorship order issued by the Church in Rome in 1553, Jewish Venetian publishers contributed hundreds of titles, popularising Renaissance ideas on humanist philosophy, medicine and religion – including the first printed Qur'an.

Interfaith Enlightenment

Leading thinkers of all faiths flocked to Ghetto's literary salons. In the 17th century, the Schola Italiana's rabbi, Leon da Modena, was so widely respected – despite his gambling habit – that Christians attended his services. When Venetian Jewish philosopher Sara Copia Sullam (1592–1641) was accused of denying the immortality of the soul – a heresy punishable by death under the Inquisition – Sullam responded with a treatise on immortality written in two days. The manifesto became a bestseller, and Sullam's writings are key works of early modern Italian literature.

Signs of Restriction

On the wall at 1131 Calle del Ghetto Vecchio, an official 1704 decree of the Republic forbids Jews who converted to Christianity from entering the Ghetto, punishable by 'the rope [hanging], prison, galleys, flogging...and other greater punishments, depending on the judgment of their excellencies (the Executors Against Blasphemy)'. These restrictions were abolished under Napoleon in 1797, when 1626 Ghetto residents gained standing as Venetian citizens.

The Enduring Legacy

Margherita Sarfatti, Mussolini's mistress from 1922 to 1938, was a Venetian Jew, and considered one of the architects of fascism in Italy. It was only when Mussolini bowed to the pressure of the Nazis and revived discriminatory rules in his 1938 Racial Laws that Sarfatti fled to Argentina. In 1943, most Jewish Venetians were deported to concentration camps. As the memorial to the northeast of the Campo del Ghetto Nuovo notes, only 37 returned. Today, few of Venice's 400-person Jewish community actually live in the Ghetto, but its legacy remains in its bookshops, art galleries and religious institutions.

Osteria di Santa Marina

VENETIAN €€€

14 MAP P122, H6

With a polished wood interior and softly lit piazza tables, this place oozes subtle class, and each course of the tasting menu brings two bites of reinvented local fare – prawn in a nest of shaved red pepper, artichoke and soft-shelled crab with squash *saor* (sweet and sour onion, pine nut and raisin marinade) – while homemade pastas marry surprising flavours such as shrimp and chestnut ravioli. Book ahead. (www.osteriadisantamarina.com)

Osteria L'Orto dei Mori

ITALIAN €€€

15 MAP P122, E3

Not since Tintoretto lived next door has this neighbourhood seen so much action thanks to this bustling and stylish restaurant. Sicilian chef Lorenzo Cipolla creates upmarket dishes, making fresh pasta daily and offering delicate delights such as squid atop *tagliolini* (ribbon pasta). Sculptural lamps set a playful mood in an artsy space with distressed, exposed brick walls. (www.osteriaortodeimori.com)

Cantina Aziende Agricole

VENETIAN €

16 MAP P122, D3

This friendly hole-in-the-wall *bacaro* (bar) serves an impressive array of local wines and draft beers to a loyal group of customers who treat the place much like a social club. Join them for a glass of Raboso and heaped platters of delicious *cicheti*, including *lardo* (cured pork fat), cheese drizzled with honey, *polpette* and deep-fried pumpkin fritters. (www.cantinaaziendeagricole.com)

Panificio Volpe Giovanni

BAKERY €

17 MAP P122, C3

In addition to unleavened pumpkin and radicchio bread, this kosher bakery sells unusual treats such as crumbly *impade* (biscuity logs flavoured with ground almonds) and *orecchiette di Amman* ('little ears of Amman'; ear-shaped pastries stuffed with chocolate), as well as excellent *cornetti*. (www.facebook.com/PanificioVolpeGiovanni)

Gelateria Ca' d'Oro

GELATO €

18 MAP P122, F5

Foot traffic stops here for spectacularly creamy or fruity gelato and zingy *granita* (crushed ice made with coffee, fresh fruit or locally grown pistachios and almonds), made in-house daily. For a summer pick-me-up, try the *granita di caffe con panna* (coffee with crushed ice and whipped cream).

Drinking

Birreria Zanon

BAR

19 MAP P122, D3

Fondamente dei Ormesini is a lively section of canal, lined with bars and *osterie*, and with its rustic

Adventures in Wine & Cicheti

Instead of a pub crawl, take a bar glide with **Row Venice** (Map p168; www.rowvenice.org). Its Cicheti Row hops between Cannaregio's canalside bars; you'll get the lowdown on Veneto varieties while learning *voga* (Venetian rowing).

If you prefer to stay on dry land for a bar hop, opt for fun and informed tours with Monica Cesarato from **Cook in Venice** (www.cookinvenice.com).

wooden seats and fishing-net decor, Birreria Zanon is a great place for a laid-back amber tipple from its craft-beer selection. There's also outdoor canalside seating. Particularly tasty are the *tramezzini* made with black bread, which go down a treat with a pint of Grimbergen amber ale. (www.facebook.com/birreriazanon/)

Marciano Pub PUB

20  MAP P122, D3

With outdoor tables overlooking the canal, and an interior that's all polished wood and gleaming taps, Maricano feels more upmarket than a pub. It stocks craft beers from around the globe, including its own brew and its samphire-infused gin. The menu is sustainably sourced burgers and steaks, including kangaroo and ostrich. There's also an oyster bar and dedicated cocktail area. (http://marcianopub.com)

Il Santo Bevitore PUB

21  MAP P122, E4

Beer lovers make pilgrimages to this canalside shrine, whose name means the 'Holy Drinker', to sample some of the 20 brews on tap, including Trappist ales and seasonal stouts. There's also a big range of speciality gin, whisky and vodka. The faithful receive canalside seating, football matches on TV, free wi-fi and the occasional live band. (www.ilsantobevitorepub.com)

Torrefazione Cannaregio CAFE

22 MAP P122, D3

With its own micro-roastery, this brick-lined cafe perched on a sunny canal bank is where to go for serious coffee, with house-made roasts including the flagship Remer, an Arabica blend with a smooth, chocolate aftertaste. For those who like more punch, there are Robusta blends, plus some delightful speciality teas. The Marchi family has been roasting since the 1930s; service is knowledgeable and friendly. (www.torrefazionecannaregio.it)

El Sbarlefo BAR

23 MAP P122, G5

All sorts sidle into this attractive little backstreet *cicheti* bar, whose name means 'the Smirk'. Visitors are drawn by an excellent wine selection and a tasty array of snacks, including light, crunchy *polpette* and loaded crostini. (www.elsbarlefo.it)

Dodo Caffè

BAR

24 MAP P122, D2

On a particularly buzzy and picturesque stretch of the Canareggio canal, Dodo offers a warm welcome, along with generously laden *cicheti* and sought-after canalside seating. (www.facebook.com/DodoCaffe)

Birre da Tutto il Mondo o Quasi

BAR

25 MAP P122, D3

The clue is in the name: 'Beers from Around the World or Almost' offers more than 100 brews, including reasonably priced bottles of craft ales and local Birra Venezia. The cheery, beery scene often spills onto the street.

Bagatela

BAR

26 MAP P122, C2

An unpretentious and popular late-night hangout on this lively stretch of canal that gets crammed with Cannaregio locals, Bagatela offers a rock soundtrack, bottled beers, cocktails, board games, sports on TV and legendary burgers made with premium Scottona beef. (www.bagatelavenezia.com)

Entertainment

Paradiso Perduto

LIVE MUSIC

27 MAP P122, E3

'Paradise Lost' is more like paradise found if you're after a cold beer and good seafood canalside on a hot summer's night. The Paradiso is particularly noted for

Watching out for High Tides

Acqua alta (high tide) isn't an emergency – it's a tide reaching 110cm above normal levels and normally happens four to six times a year, between November and April. *Acqua alta* may cause flooding in low-lying areas, but waters usually recede within five hours.

To see if *acqua alta* is likely, check Venice's Centro Maree 48-hour tidal forecast at www.comune.venezia.it. Alarm tones sound when *acqua alta* is expected to reach the city within two to four hours:

- One even tone (up to 110cm above normal): barely warrants a pause in happy-hour conversation.
- Two rising tones (110cm to 120cm): you might need *stivali di gomma* (rubber boots).
- Three rising tones (around 130cm): check Centro Maree online to see where *passarelle* (gangplank walkways) are in use.
- Four rising tones (140cm and up): businesses may close early.

its Monday-night gigs; Chet Baker, Keith Richards and Vinicio Capossela have all played the small stage. (https://ilparadisoperduto.wordpress.com/)

Casinò Di Venezia CASINO

28 MAP P122, D4

Founded in 1638, the world's oldest casino moved into its current palatial home in the 1950s: taking on the house (spoiler, it usually wins) has never looked so glamorous. You can dress casually for the slots, but don your jacket and poker face for gaming tables. Arrive in style with a free water-taxi ride from Piazzale Roma. You must be at least 18 to enter the casino. (www.casinovenezia.it)

Ca' Macana Atelier

ABIGAIL BLASI ©

Shopping

Ca' Macana Atelier ARTS & CRAFTS

29 MAP P122, D3

Resist buying mass-produced Carnevale masks until you've checked out the traditionally made papier-mâché and leather masks at this treasure-trove shop and workshop. Reproduction vintage prints of Venice are another good buy. (www.camacana.com)

Gianni Basso STATIONERY

30 MAP P122, H5

A traditional printer's workshop, at this charming shop you can order your own custom-made writing paper, invitations and cards. You can also buy exquisite readymade printed cards. Trained at the Armenian Monastery, Gianni is as much a piece of Venetian history as his miniature print museum next door.

Vittorio Costantini GLASS

31 MAP P122, H5

This glassware is very much for the serious collector. With a focus on the natural world, these are works of art: magical, miniature insects, butterflies, shells and birds that Vittorio Costantini fashions out of glass using a lampwork technique. Some of the iridescent beetles have bodies made of 21 segments that need to be fused together with dazzling dexterity and speed. (www.vittoriocostantini.com)

L'Isola di Pinocchio

GIFTS & SOUVENIRS

32 MAP P122, E4

Ring a bell to gain access to this 1st-floor workshop, hung with Roberto Comin's extraordinary puppets, which are collectables rather than toys (prices start at €200). Comin could not look more the part, as if Geppetto (Pinocchio's creator) has come to life. Comin makes the puppets and his sister makes the clothes. (www.marionettesinvenice.com)

Balducci Borse

SHOES

33 MAP P122, D4

Step through the door of Franco Balducci's Cannaregio workshop and you can smell the quality of the hand-picked Tuscan hides that he fashions on the premises into women's boots and glossy shoulder bags. (www.balducciborse.com)

Leonardo

JEWELLERY

34 MAP P122, D4

Hiding in plain sight on touristy Strada Nova, this authentic Murano glass shop stocks jewellery from some of Venice's very best glass artists, many of whom rarely sell outside their own showrooms. Chalcedony pendants in opal glass by Antonio Vaccari and contemporary statement necklaces by Igor Balbi are complemented by unique historical pieces.

Dressing for Carnevale

Nicolao Atelier (Map p122, E3; www.nicolao.com) is where to source your exquisitely handmade Carnevale glad rags, if you have a budget of a few hundred euros. In his past life, Stefano Nicolao was an actor and assistant costumier before finding his true calling as a scholar and curator of historical fashion, over 10,000 pieces of which are now stored in his vast studio.

Antichità al Ghetto

ANTIQUES

35 MAP P122, C3

Take home a memento of Venetian history from this antiques shop: an ancient map of the canal, holy silverware, an etching of Venetian dandies daintily alighting from gondolas or an 18th-century cameo once worn by the most fashionable ladies of the Ghetto. (www.antichitaalghetto.com)

Explore Castello

Stretching eastwards from San Marco, Castello is the city's largest neighbourhood, containing the ancient Arsenale shipyards that Dante used as inspiration for hell, alongside frescoed orphanages where Vivaldi conducted, and avant-garde Biennale pavilions. At the tip of Venice's tail is a pine-shaded park where Venetians go to escape their extraordinary inner city.

The Short List

- ***La Pietà (p147)*** *Experiencing a classical concert on the site where Vivaldi was once concertmaster to an orchestra of orphans.*
- ***Riva degli Schiavoni (p137)*** *Catching sunset along Castello's picturesque waterfront promenade.*
- ***Palazzo Grimani (p140)*** *Viewing classical statuary returned to this extraordinary Renaissance palazzo (mansion).*
- ***La Biennale di Venezia (p142)*** *Pondering modern art and ground-breaking architecture in the Arsenale and Giardini Pubblici.*
- ***Scuola Dalmata di San Giorgio degli Schiavoni (p140)*** *Basking in the golden glow of Carpaccio's paintings in this Dalmatian confraternity house.*

Getting There & Around

Vaporetto Castello is encircled with *vaporetto* stops. Lines 4.1 and 4.2 stop at all of them; 5.1 and 5.2 stop at all but Arsenale. Line 1 makes all the southern stops, linking them to the Grand Canal and the Lido.

Castello Map on p138

Arsenale (p140) JAN CATTANEO/SHUTTERSTOCK ©

Walking Tour

Castello's Byways

Leave the crowds and cramped quarters of San Marco behind, and stretch your legs on a sunny stroll through Castello, where saints and sailors come with the territory.

Walk Facts

Start Zanipolo (Chiesa di SS Giovanni e Paolo); *vaporetto* Ospedale

Finish Giardini Pubblici; *vaporetto* Giardini

Length 6.5km; three hours

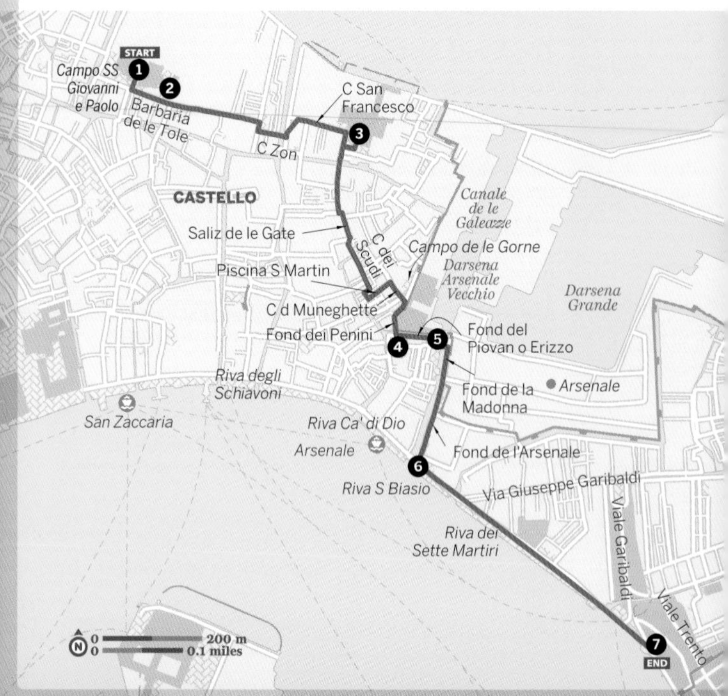

❶ Zanipolo

Rising above Castello's tallest ship masts is the unfinished, vast Gothic **Zanipolo** (p143) basilica. Its 33m-high nave provides a fitting setting for 25 doges' tombs.

❷ Ospedaletto

Upstaging the Zanipolo exterior is marble-lined statue-bedecked **Ospedaletto**, a 1660s orphanage designed by Longhena. This refuge was once famed for its orchestra of orphan girls; today it functions as an elder-care facility.

❸ Chiesa di San Francesco della Vigna

Continue down Barbaria de le Tole, cross Ca' Zon bridge, then dog-leg left to see Palladio-colonnaded **Chiesa di San Francesco della Vigna** (p140), where Antonio Negroponte's Madonna and child float like a hovercraft above Venice's lagoon.

❹ Chiesa di San Martino

Heading south, you'll bump into the massive walls of the **Arsenale** (p140), Venice's legendary shipyard. Turn right at Campo de le Gorne and follow the walls to the **church** dedicated to St Martin, patron saint of wine and soldiers. By the doorway is a *bocca di leoni* (mouth of the lion), a slot where Venetians slipped denunciations of their neighbours. *Arsenalotti* (Arsenale workers) were sworn to silence about trade secrets, since loose lips could sink ships – so reckless talk in Castello bars could be reported as high treason, punishable by death.

❺ Porta Magna

The Arsenale's **main gate** is considered the city's earliest Renaissance structure. By the 18th century naval production at the Arsenale had dwindled and the republic was in terminal decline. In 1797 La Serenissima surrendered to Napoleon without a fight.

❻ Riva

From **Riva degli Schiavoni**, turn south onto Castello's breathtaking waterfront promenade to admire sweeping views across the lagoon.

❼ Giardini Pubblici

The tree-shaded Napoleonic **public gardens** (p140) are dotted with Biennale pavilions, and thronged in summer and autumn with artists, architects and admirers from around the world. Between Biennales you can still enjoy the rest of the park.

Take a Break

After your walk, enjoy a heavenly herbal tisane inside Napoleon's handsome greenhouse at Serra dei Giardini (p146) – or a sailor-size *spritz* (prosecco cocktail) and lagoon-front seat to watch boats drift past at **Paradiso** (Map p138, H6; www.inparadiso.net).

A
B
C
D
1
2
3
4
5
6
Gelataria Ducale
Campo SS Giovanni e Paolo
8 Zanipolo
Saliz S Zanipolo
26
Rio di San Marina
Rio di S Lio
C del Dose
Campo Santa Marina
C Bressane
21
Osteria di Santa Marina
34 Campo San Lio
33
C Carminati
C Pindemonte
C Lunga Santa Maria Formosa
C de l'Ospedale
Barbaria de le Tole
Fond Moro
Rio de la Tetta
C de le Capucine
Rio di Santa Giustina
C San Francesco
C Zon
C d Tedeum
Rio di San Francesco
C Mondo Novo
Fond dei Preti
35
C dei Orbi
11 Reali Wellness Spa
Saliz San Lio
Campo Santa Maria Formosa
Palazzo Grimani
1
Campo San Lorenzo
Borgoloco San Lorenzo
C di Morion
Corte Nova
Campo della Fava
30
16
7
Fondazione Querini Stampalia
Ruga Giuffa
C di Mezzo
Rio di San Severo
Rio di San Lorenzo
Scuola Dalmata di San Giorgio degli Schiavoni
4
C de la Guerra
C Querini
C d Magazen
18
C d Madonna
C Lion
C dei Furlani
Fond dei Furlani
C dei Spechieri
C Fiubera
C d Corona
32
Museo delle Icone
9
17
C d Chiesa
C d Figher
CASTELLO
Campiello dei Greci
Saliz dei Greci
C de l'Arco
Gondola Service
27
C del Pestrin
C d Selvadego
Saliz San Provolo
6
Rio dei Greci
Campo Bandiera e Moro
14
Piazza San Marco
C dei Albanesi
20
Rio del Vin
Campo San Zaccaria
Chiesa di San Zaccaria
Rio de la Pietà
SAN MARCO
C delle Rasse
23
25
19
La Pietà
Cllo d Pescaria
15
28
Riva degli Schiavoni
San Zaccaria A
Riva degli Schiavoni
Rio dei Giardinetti
San Zaccaria
San Zaccaria C/D
San Zaccaria B
Giardini Reali
San Marco Giardinetti
Bacino di San Marco
San Giorgio Maggiore
Campo San Giorgio
Isola di San Giorgio Maggiore

E
F
G
H
Canale de le Fondamente Nuove
0 400 m
0 0.2 miles
For reviews see
Sights p140
Eating p143
Drinking p145
Entertainment p147
Shopping p148
Celestia
Chiesa di San Francesco della Vigna
5
C Sagredo
C San Francesco
Campo della Celestia
Campo S Ternità
C de l'Ogio
Rio del Scudi
Canale de le Galeazze
C Magno
Rio de le Gorne
Darsena Arsenale Vecchio
Darsena Grande
C Venier
Rio de le Vergini
Fond de la Madonna
12
29
Campo de l'Arsenal
C d Erizzo
10
Padiglione delle Navi
Arsenale
3
Rio di San Gerolamo
Saliz Stretta
Fond Riello
Rio Ca' di Dio
C dei Forni
Rio de l'Arsenale
Fond de l'Arsenale
Riva Ca' di Dio
Campo de la Tana
Rio de la Tana
Fond de la Tana
Arsenale
C Fianco la Chiesa d S Biagio
C dei Preti
13
Campo S Biasio
Fond di San Gioacchin
Fond di Sant'Anna
31
C Crosera
Via Giuseppe Garibaldi
24
C Coboto
C de le Ancore
C G B Tiepolo
C Correra
C San Domenico
Viale Garibaldi
Riva dei Sette Martiri
C Colonne
C Schiavona
Saresin
Corte
Seco Marina
Fond San Isepo
Bacino di San Marco
22
Rio di San Giuseppe
Cte d Solda
Viale Trento
Giardini
Giardini Pubblici
2
La Biennale di Venezia
Playground Paradiso
1
2
3
4
5
6
Castello

Sights

Palazzo Grimani MUSEUM

1 MAP P138, B2

The Grimani family built their Renaissance *palazzo* in 1568 to showcase the extraordinary Graeco-Roman sculpture collection of Cardinal Giovanni Grimani. The palace has some incredible ceilings, including Roman-inspired stucco and the remarkable foliage room. Most spectacular of all is the Tribuna, whose inlay and Pantheon-style oculus provide an incredible setting for their original antiquities, returned from Museo Correr (p54) in 2019 – after a 430-year absence. (www.palazzogrimani.org)

Giardini Pubblici GARDENS

2 MAP P138, H6

Begun under Napoleon as the city's first public green space, these leafy gardens are the main home of Venice's Biennale. Around half of the gardens is open to the public all year round; the rest is given over to the permanent **Biennale pavilions**, each representing a different country. Many of them are attractions in their own right, from Carlo Scarpa's daring 1954 raw-concrete-and-glass Venezuelan Pavilion to Denton Corker Marshall's 2015 Australian Pavilion in black granite.

Arsenale HISTORIC SITE

3 MAP P138, F4

Founded in 1104, the Arsenale became the greatest medieval shipyard in Europe, home to 300 shipping companies employing up to 16,000 people. Dante evoked it as a site for boiling pitch in his *Inferno*. Capable of turning out a new galley in a day, it is considered a forerunner of mass industrial production. Access is only possible during major events and exhibitions such as Carnevale, the Arte Laguna Prize and the art and architecture Biennale, when its hulking workshops and warehouses make for awe-inspiring exhibition spaces. (www.labiennale.org/en/venues/arsenale)

Scuola Dalmata di San Giorgio degli Schiavoni CHURCH

4 MAP P138, D3

This 15th-century Dalmatian religious-confraternity house is dedicated to favourite Slavic saints George, Tryphon and Jerome. It was one of the few schools not to be supressed by Napoleon. The saints' lives are captured with precision and glowing early-Renaissance grace by 15th-century master Vittore Carpaccio. To see these and the Renaissance interior – one of Venice's best preserved – book ahead, as visits are by guided tour and appointment only. (www.scuoladalmatavenezia.com)

Chiesa di San Francesco della Vigna CHURCH

5 MAP P138, E2

Designed and built by Jacopo Sansovino, with a facade by Palladio, this enchanting Franciscan church is one of Venice's most under-appreciated attractions. The Madonna positively glows in Bellini's *Madonna and Saints* (1507) in the **Cappella Santa**, just off the flower-carpeted cloister, while swimming angels and strutting birds steal the scene in the delightful *Virgin and Child Enthroned* (c 1455) by Antonio da Negroponte, near the door to the right of the sanctuary.

Chiesa di San Zaccaria CHURCH

6 MAP P138, C3

When 15th-century Venetian girls showed more interest in sailors than saints, they were sent to the convent adjoining San Zaccaria. The wealth showered on the church by their grateful parents is evident. Masterpieces by Bellini, Titian, Tintoretto and Van Dyck crowd the walls. The star of the show is undoubtedly Giovanni Bellini's *Madonna Enthroned with Child and Saints* (1505), which graces an altar on the left as you enter, and glows like it's plugged into an outlet.

Fondazione Querini Stampalia MUSEUM

7 MAP P138, B2

In 1869 Conte Giovanni Querini Stampalia left his ancestral 16th-century *palazzo* to the city on the condition that the bequest, including the 700-year-old library, were put to public use. Part of the preserved rooms give an insight into the lifestyle of the

Castello waterfront

La Biennale di Venezia

The world's most prestigious arts show is something of a misnomer: the **Venice Biennale** (Map p138, H6; www.labiennale.org) is actually held every year, but the spotlight alternates between art (odd-numbered years) and architecture (even years). The April to November art biennial presents contemporary art at 29 national pavilions in the Giardini Pubblici (p140), with additional exhibitions in venues across town. The architecture biennial is usually held mid-May to November, filling vast Arsenale boat sheds with high-concept structures.

The History of the Biennale

Venice held its first Biennale in 1895 to reassert its role as global taste-maker and provide an essential corrective to the brutality of the Industrial Revolution. At first the Biennale retained strict control, removing a provocative Picasso from the Spanish Pavilion in 1910, but after WWII, national pavilions asserted their autonomy and the Biennale became an international avant-garde showcase.

The Pavilions

The Biennale's 29 pavilions tell a fascinating story of 20th-century architecture reflecting national identities from Hungary's futuristic folklore hut to Canada's ski-lodge cathedral. The most recent addition is the 2015 Australian Pavilion by starchitects Denton Corker Marshall. The black granite box hidden amid the foliage speaks of the imposition of European settlements on Indigenous Australian lands.

Beyond the Biennale

The city-backed Biennale organisation also runs the Venice International Film Festival in September and organises an International Festival of Contemporary Dance and concert series in summer. For upcoming events check the website. To defray substantial costs to the city, there's an entry fee to the main art and architecture shows and film festival premieres – but many ancillary arts programs are free. When the art biennale's in town, book two months ahead for accommodation, and at least a week ahead at popular Castello restaurants.

19th-century Venetian aristocracy, with an art collection including works by Tintoretto and Canaletto, while downstairs is Carlo Scarpa's modernist garden and an adjoining cafe. The boutique onsite sells some lovely glassware and jewellery. (www.querinistampalia.it)

Zanipolo BASILICA

8 MAP P138, B1

Commenced in 1333 but not finished until the 1430s, and with much brickwork left exposed, this vast church is similar in style and scope to the Franciscan Frari in San Polo, which was being raised at the same time. Both oversized structures feature red-brick facades with high-contrast detailing in white stone. After its completion, Zanipolo quickly became the go-to church for ducal funerals and inside you'll find 25 of their lavish tombs. There's a small entry fee. (www.basilicasantigiovanniepaolo.it)

Museo delle Icone MUSEUM

9 MAP P138, C3

Glowing colours, irridescent medieval manuscripts, and all-seeing eyes fill this treasure box of some 80 Byzantine-style icons made in 14th- to 17th-century Italy, inherited from the Greek Orthodox Venetian community. Look out for the expressive *San Giovanni Climaco*, which shows the saintly author of a Greek spiritual guide distracted from his work by visions of souls diving into hell. (www.istitutoellenico.org)

Padiglione delle Navi MUSEUM

10 MAP P138, E4

A boat lover's dream, the Padiglione delle Navi is a vast 2000 sq metre warehouse containing spectacular, gilded Venetian boats, including historic luggers, gondolas, racing boats, military vessels, a funerary barge and a royal motorboat. It's an annexe of the **Museo Storico Navale**. (www.visitmuve.it)

Reali Wellness Spa SPA

11 MAP P138, A2

In this surprisingly spa-starved city, the Hotel ai Reali's wellness centre offers a mosaicked, scented sanctuary on the top floor, where light floods into the Turkish bath. There's a range of Thai massages, facials and treatments to relieve leg fatigue: useful after walking across Venice's myriad bridges. (www.hotelaireali.com)

Eating

Trattoria Corte Sconta VENETIAN €€€

12 MAP P138, E3

Sit in the sun-dappled, vine-shaded *corte sconta* (hidden courtyard) to dine on seafood antipasti and imaginative house-made pasta, such as black seafood spaghetti. Inventive flavour pairings transform the classics: clams zing with ginger, and prawn and courgette linguine is recast with an earthy dash of saffron. (www.cortescontavenezia.it)

Salvmeria VENETIAN €

13 MAP P138, F5

Fashioned from an old deli, with the name the original sign, Marco Ginepri's cool *cichetteria* (tapas restaurant) serves accomplished food and excellent Veneto wines.

Gourmet *cicheti* (Venetian tapas) include fluffy *baccalá* (cod) on polenta, marinated shrimps and Fassone beef with peppers, while main plates include succulent tuna in a sesame crust, warm potato salad with radicchio and belly-warming fish lasagne. Trust them to recommend interesting wine pairings. (www.salvmeria.com)

CoVino

VENETIAN **€€**

14 MAP P138, D3

You'll need to reserve ahead for tiny CoVino, which has only 14 seats but demonstrates bags of ambition with its inventive, seasonal menu inspired by the Venetian terroir. Speciality products are selected from Slow Food Foundation producers, and the charming waiters make enthusiastic recommendations from the wine list. (www.covinovenezia.com)

Al Covo

VENETIAN **€€€**

15 MAP P138, D4

Smart, with gleaming white tablecloths on the indoor and outdoor tables, this is a cut-above restaurant where Cesare Benelli has long been dedicated to the preservation of heritage products and lagoon recipes. Only the freshest seasonal fish gets the Covo treatment, accompanied by artichokes, eggplant, *cipollini* onion and mushrooms from the lagoon larders of Sant'Erasmus, Vignole, Treporti and Cavallino. Meat is also carefully sourced and much of it is Slow Food accredited. (www.ristorantealcovo.com)

Al Covo

Alle Testiere

VENETIAN €€€

16 MAP P138, B2

Make a reservation to ensure a table at this tiny restaurant and come prepared for Bruno Gavagnin's beautifully plated seafood feasts, with spices and scents that recall Venice's trading past with the East, with delicate dishes such as scallops with orange and summer leeks. (www.osterialletestiere.it)

Local

VENETIAN €€€

17 MAP P138, D3

In a gracious, contemporary dining room with a wrought-iron-framed arched window, Local's chef Salvatore Sodano gives a creative twist to classic, ancient Venetian recipes, such as risotto with *gò*, a recipe invented in Burano in the 16th century, made from goby fish from the lagoon. At lunch there's a four-course menu, with optional wine pairings, while at dinner choose from a seven- or nine-course tasting menu. (www.ristorantelocal.com)

Al Giardinetto da Severino

VENETIAN €€

18 MAP P138, C3

Al Giardinetto's romantic, vine-covered courtyard is a welcome surprise in this warren of backstreets, while its interior is the former chapel of 15th-century Palazzo Zorzi. For nearly 70 years the Bastianello-Parmesan family have been serving up traditional dishes here, such as crab pasta and veal schnitzel. (www.algiardinetto.it)

Wildner

VENETIAN €€€

19 MAP P138, C4

In a glass pavilion on the Riva degli Schiavoni, Pensione Wildner's restaurant has been open since the 1960s and – now under the auspices of nearby Local – serves well-executed traditional Venetian dishes, such as risotto with *gò* and octopus on lentils. The prime waterfront position makes it a perfect place for lunch. (www.hotelwildner.com)

Trattoria alla Rivetta

VENETIAN €€

20 MAP P138, B3

Tucked behind the Ponte San Provolo, this wood-lined trattoria hums with the chatter of contented diners even in the dead of winter. It is staffed by a clutch of jovial waiters in equally jovial red waistcoats, who'll cordially serve you platters of lagoon fare such as spaghetti alle vongole, tagliolini with crab or *fritto misto* (mixed fried seafood).

Drinking

Osteria Al Portego

BAR

21 MAP P138, A2

This convivial walk-in closet somehow manages to distribute wine, craft beer and *cicheti* to the crowd of young Venetians in approximate order of arrival. There's a selection of prosecco, reds and whites by the glass, the bar groans with crostini, and punters overflow onto a few chairs outside. If you fancy something more substantial, in the back there are six sought-after tables where you can eat fried seafood or risotto. (www.osteriaalportego.org)

Serra dei Giardini

CAFE

22 MAP P138, G5

This is a lovely, tranquil spot for a coffee, hot chocolate or pastry, with sun-shaded tables in the garden of a grand belle-époque greenhouse, built in 1894 to house the palms used in Biennale events, and which quickly became a social hub and a centre for propagation: many plants grown here adorned the municipal flowerbeds of the Lido and the ballrooms of aristocratic *palazzi*, and you can still browse the lush garden centre. (www.serradeigiardini.org)

Serra dei Giardini

Bar Terrazza Danieli

BAR

23 MAP P138, B4

For romance and top-end tipples, you can't ask for better than this balcony bar. Gondolas glide in to dock along the quay, the lagoon turns to teal, and across the water, the white marble of Palladio's San Giorgio Maggiore turns rose gold and pink in the waters of the canal. (www.danielihotelvenice.com)

El Rèfolo

BAR

24 MAP P138, F5

A gem among the touristy bars along Via Garibaldi, spot El Rèfolo by the crowd of locals at its pavement tables. Friendly waiters dispense Italian microbrews and glasses of wine, as well as delicious *cicheti*. (www.elrefolo.it)

Bar Dandolo

COCKTAIL BAR

25 MAP P138, B4

Dress to the nines and swan straight past the 'hotel guests only' sign to the glamorous grand waterfront hall of the 14th-century Palazzo Dandolo, with antique windows framing Grand Canal views. Sink into plush tub chairs under glorious Murano chandeliers that glitter like ice, while snappily dressed staff whisk you whatever you fancy from a range of high-end cocktails, such as signature Vesper martinis. (www.marriott.it)

Vivaldi's Orphan Orchestra

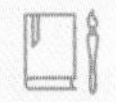

Over the centuries, Venetian musicians developed a reputation for playing as though their lives depended on it – which at times wasn't far from the truth. With shrinking 17th-century trade revenues, the state took the quixotic step of underwriting musical education for orphan girls, and the investment produced surprising returns.

Among the maestri hired to conduct orphan-girl orchestras was Antonio Vivaldi (1678–1741), whose 30-year tenure yielded hundreds of concertos and popularised Venetian baroque music across Europe. Visitors spread word of extraordinary performances by orphan girls, and the city became a magnet for novelty-seeking, moneyed socialites.

Modern visitors to Venice can still see music and opera performed in the same venues as in Vivaldi's day – including Tiepolo-frescoed **La Pietà** (Map p138, C4; www.pietavenezia.org), the *ospedaletto* (orphanage) where Vivaldi was the musical director.

Rosa Salva

CAFE

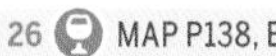

26 MAP P138, B1

For over a century, Rosa Salva has been serving tea, pastries and ice creams on sociable Campo Zanipolo. The 1930s interior is a perfect setting to nibble on *tramezzini* (triangular, stacked sandwiches) and trays of *tè con limone* (tea with lemon) at marble-topped tables while, outside, people-watching sunseekers sip *spritz* and children slurp ice creams. (www.rosasalva.it)

Bacaro Risorto

BAR

27 MAP P138, C3

Just a footbridge away from San Marco, this convivial shoebox of a corner bar overflows with happy drinkers sipping quality wines, *spritz* and grazing on abundant *cicheti* (Venetian tapas), including crostini heaped with *sarde in saor* (sardines in a sweet and sour sauce).

Entertainment

Collegium Ducale

CLASSICAL MUSIC

28 MAP P138, B4

Spend an enjoyable evening in prison with this six-member chamber orchestra, which performs Vivaldi's *Four Seasons* in the grand hall of the Prison's Palace, rather than in the cells. On alternate nights opera singers tackle everything from Mozart to Gershwin accompanied only by a piano. (www.collegiumducale.com)

Shopping

Atelier Alessandro Merlin

HOMEWARES

29 MAP P138, E3

Alessandro Merlin paints striking, mostly monochrome sea life, animals and well-endowed nudes on white ceramics. They're more work of art than everyday items. The sgraffito technique Alessandro uses on some of his work dates back to Roman times.

Kalimala

SHOES

30 MAP P138, A2

With a shop full of hand-made gladiator or slip-on sandals, boots, belts, bags, sandals and gloves, the friendly team at Kalimala makes beautiful leather goods in practical, modern styles. All are crafted from vegetable-cured cowhide and dyed in a mix of earthy tones and vibrant lapis blues. Given the natural tanning and top-flight leather, prices are extremely reasonable. (https://kalimala.net)

Kirumakata

JEWELLERY

31 MAP P138, H5

Striking, contemporary statement jewellery fashioned from Murano glass by Alessandra Gardin, at reasonable prices. This small shop sells beautiful earrings, bracelets, necklaces and cufflinks, and you can see work ongoing on pieces at the back of the shop. (www.kirumakata.com)

Bar Terrazza Danieli (p146)

Paolo Brandolisio ARTS & CRAFTS

32 MAP P138, C3

Beneath all the marble and gilt, Venice is a city of wood, long supported by its carpenters, caulkers, oar-makers and gilders. Master woodcarver Paolo Brandolisio continues the traditions, crafting the sinuous *forcola* (rowlock) that supports the gondolier's oar. Made of walnut or cherry wood, each is crafted specifically for boat and gondolier. Miniature replicas are for sale in the workroom.

Ma Va' Collection CLOTHING

33 MAP P138, A2

To be as elegant as the true Venetians, head to the boutique of Ma (Marianna) and Va' (Valentina), with beautifully crafted clothing for men and women in muted colours, with chic details and gorgeous cut. This is subtly brilliant clothing to create a *bella figura* (beautiful look; essential in Italy). (www.mavacollection.com)

Giovanna Zanella SHOES

34 MAP P138, A2

Woven, sculpted and crested like lagoon birds, Zanella's shoes practically demand that red carpets roll out before you. The Venetian designer custom-makes shoes, so the answer is always: yes, you can get those peep-toe numbers in yellow and grey, size 12, extra narrow. They take a few weeks to make and she'll send you the finished pair. Prices start at €850 a pair. (www.giovannazanella.com)

Local Food Favourites

I love Serra dei Giardini (p146). It's a Liberty-style building, with a bar, and it's in a green area, very peaceful. There's a plant and flower shop, and afterwards you can go to the park, the green part of Venice.

My favourite restaurant in Castello is Osteria di Santa Marina (p129). Prices are a little higher, but everything is special.

I love ice cream, and I think Venice's best is Gelataria Ducale (p127). The owner had a cake shop for 15 years, and now she makes very good ice cream.

Recommended by Giovanna Zanella, *designer shoe-maker*

Artigianato Veneziano JEWELLERY

35 MAP P138, B2

Using traditional Murano techniques and materials, including oxides and resins, Sabina Melinato, a teacher at Murano's International School of Glass, conjures up contemporary costume jewellery. Her art-deco-inspired glass pendants are so highly polished they look like lacquerwork. She also stocks other local designers.

Explore

Giudecca, Lido & the Southern Islands

Where other cities have urban sprawl, Venice has a teal-blue lagoon dotted with mirage-like islands and rare wildlife. To the south, the islands are only a short vaporetto hop away. Giudecca was once the getaway of the Venice elite, later a military industrial complex, and now a centre for Venice's creatives. Only one stop away is the cultural hub of Isola di San Giorgio Maggiore, with its magnificent church, while the laidback Lido is where Venice goes to the beach.

The Short List

- ***Basilica di San Giorgio Maggiore (p152)*** *Immersing yourself in the serenity of Palladio's eye-catching church and ascending its bell tower for spectacular San Marco views.*
- ***La Palanca (p158)*** *Enjoying a waterside lunch after visiting the art and artisans taking over Giudecca's cloisters and warehouses.*
- ***Fondazione Giorgio Cini (p157)*** *Taking in Palladio's cloister, Longhena's library and an elaborate garden maze on the Isola di San Giorgio Maggiore.*

Getting There & Around

Vaporetto Giudecca: lines 2, 4.1, 4.2 and N (night) from San Marco or Dorsoduro; San Giorgio Maggiore: line 2 from San Zaccaria and San Marco; Lido: lines 1, 2, 10 from San Marco, 2, 5.1, 5.2 and 14 from San Zaccaria, and 6 and 8 from Zattere.

Guidecca, Lido & the Southern Islands Map on p156

Giudecca PERFEKOTYPOLE/SHUTTERSTOCK ©

Top Experience

Savour the View from Basilica di San Giorgio Maggiore

Designed by Andrea Palladio for maximum dazzle, this Benedictine abbey church was built between 1565 and 1610 and positioned on its own island, facing San Marco. Palladio chose white Istrian stone to stand out against the blue waters of the lagoon and set it at an angle to create visual drama while also ensuring that it catches the sun all afternoon.

MAP P156, D1

www.abbaziasangiorgio.it

Palladio's Facade

Palladio's radical facade gracefully solved the problem bedevilling Renaissance church design: how to graft a triangular, classical pediment onto a Christian church with a high, central nave and lower side aisles. Palladio's solution: use one pediment to crown the nave and a lower half-pediment to span each side aisle. The two interlock with rhythmic harmony, while prominent three-quarter columns, deeply incised capitals and sculptural niches create depth with clever shadow-play. Above the facade rises a brick *campanile* (bell tower) with a conical copper spire and a cap of Istrian stone.

Interior

The interior is an uncanny combination of brightness and serenity. Sunlight enters through high thermal windows and is then diffused by acres of white stucco. Floors inlaid with white, red and black stone draw the eye toward the altar. With its rigorous application of classical motifs, it's reminiscent of a Roman theatre.

Tintorettos

Two outstanding late works by Tintoretto flank the church's altar. On one side hangs his *Collection of Manna;* on the other side, his *Last Supper* depicts Christ and the apostles in a scene that looks suspiciously like a 16th-century Venetian tavern, with a cat and a dog angling for scraps. Nearby hangs what is considered to be Tintoretto's final masterpiece, the moving *Deposition of Christ.*

★ Top Tips

- Take the lift to the top of the bell tower, where you can catch a unique view back across the lagoon; it's an astounding panorama and you won't have to queue.
- Tintoretto's final work, the *Deposition of Christ* (1594), hangs in the Cappella delle Deposizione, which is accessed from the sanctuary but is only open for Mass.

Take a Break

There's nowhere to eat on the island itself, so jump on the *vaporetto* to Giudecca (line 2) for a quick bite at La Palanca (p158).

For a more upmarket meal, try Trattoria ai Cacciatori (p159).

Cycling Tour

Cycling Around the Lido

The 11km-long sandbar is lined with beaches on the seaward side. For much of it, you have to pay for a space, but there is a section of free beach. Cars are allowed, which is something of a shock, but roads aren't busy and it's a great place to cycle.
The sleepy Lido turns to Hollywood during September's film festival, which takes place at the Palazzo del Cinema (Map p156, E4; www.labiennale.org)

Cycling Facts

Start Lido on Bike; *vaporetto* Lido SME

Finish Pachuka; bus A

Length 3km; 1½ hours

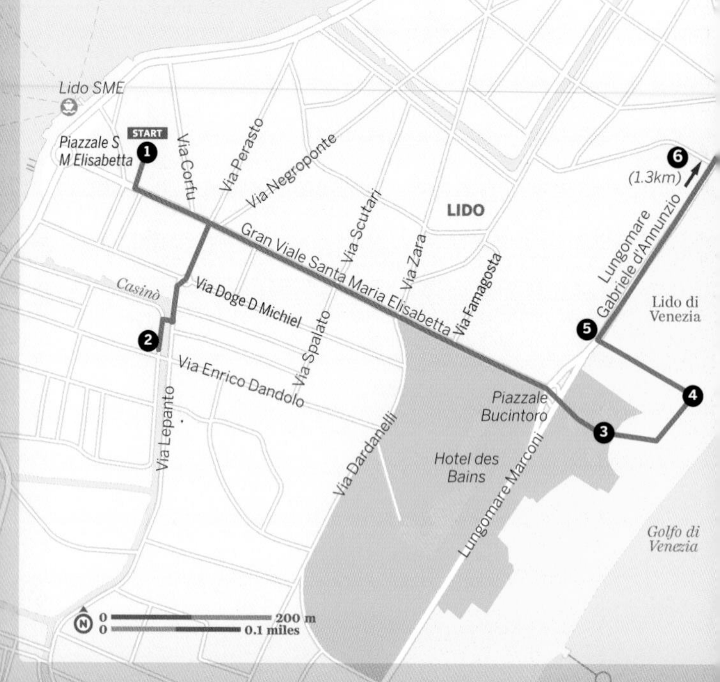

❶ Lido on Bike

To tour at your own pace, you can rent a lovely smart bike or four-person surrey from friendly **Lido on Bike** (www.lidoonbike.it) at exceedingly reasonable rates. Identification showing you're at least 18 is required.

❷ Al Mercà

Located in the old Lido fish market, lovely **al Mercà** (www.osteriaalmerca.it) is a local hub and year-round draw for its abundant *cicheti* (Venetian tapas), outdoor seating and well-priced wine by the glass. Take a pew at one of the marble counters and order up a seafood storm of *folpetti* (mini octopus), fried *schìe* (shrimp) and creamy salt cod.

❸ Blue Moon

From afar, the domed semicircular structure of **Blue Moon** looks like an alien landing. It encompasses a bar and beach restaurant that has live music and DJ events in the summer. You can also rent umbrellas and sunbeds from here.

❹ Public Beach

A relaxing, soft-sanded place to escape the city and pretend you're on a beach holiday, the *spiaggia comunale* (public beach) next to the Lido's ferry stop gets busy on sunny weekends, as you don't have to pay for a sunbed here.

❺ El Pecador

No, you're not suffering from heatstroke: that really is a red double-decker bus parked along the Lungomare, attracting an alternative crowd to impromptu beach parties. Head to **El Pecador** for some of the Lido's finest stuffed sandwiches and *spritz* (prosecco cocktails) and claim a seat on the canopied top deck.

❻ Pachuka

The most reliable of the Lido's summertime dance spots, **Pachuka** works year-round as a snack bar and pizzeria, but on weekend nights in summer it cranks up as a beachside dance club, too. Expect live music and DJ sets right on the beach.

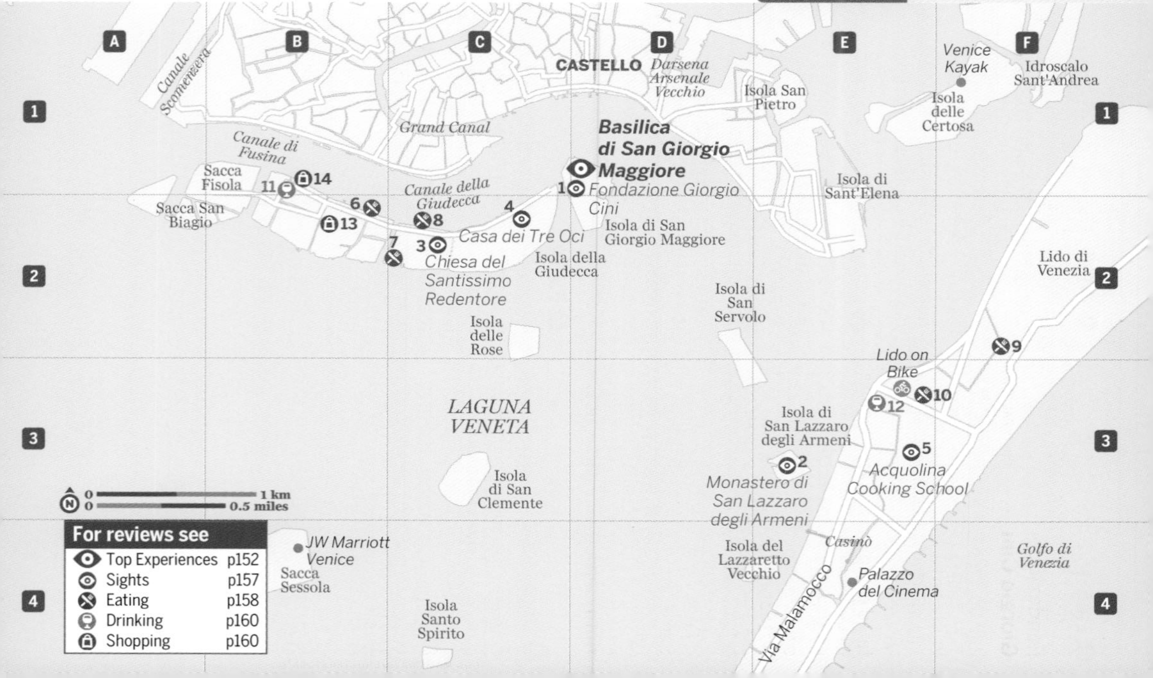

A B C D E F
1 2 3 4

CASTELLO
Darsena Arsenale Vecchio
Isola San Pietro
Isola di Sant'Elena
Isola delle Certosa
Venice Kayak
Idroscalo Sant'Andrea
Lido di Venezia
Grand Canal
Canale di Fusina
Canale Scomenzera
Sacca Fisola
Sacca San Biagio
Canale della Giudecca
Basilica di San Giorgio Maggiore
1 Fondazione Giorgio Cini
Isola di San Giorgio Maggiore
Isola della Giudecca
4 Casa dei Tre Oci
3 Chiesa del Santissimo Redentore
Isola delle Rose
Isola di San Servolo
LAGUNA VENETA
Isola di San Clemente
Isola Santo Spirito
JW Marriott Venice
Sacca Sessola
Isola di San Lazzaro degli Armeni
2 Monastero di San Lazzaro degli Armeni
Isola del Lazzaretto Vecchio
Lido on Bike
5 Acquolina Cooking School
Casinò
Palazzo del Cinema
Via Malamocco
Golfo di Venezia
6 7 8 9 10 11 12 13 14

0 — 1 km
0 — 0.5 miles

For reviews see

Top Experiences	p152
Sights	p157
Eating	p158
Drinking	p160
Shopping	p160

Sights

Fondazione Giorgio Cini CULTURAL CENTRE

1 MAP P156, D1

In 1951, industrialist and art patron Vittorio Cini acquired the monastery of San Giorgio. The rehabilitated complex is an architectural treasure incorporating designs by Andrea Palladio and Baldassare Longhena, and includes an **outdoor theatre** that Katherine Hepburn called the 'most beautiful in the world'. You need to book the differently themed tours online. Some visit the cloisters, some the refectory and libraries and then gaze down on the **Borges Labyrinth** – an intricate garden maze built to honour Argentinian writer Jorge Luis Borges. (www.cini.it)

Monastero di San Lazzaro degli Armeni MONASTERY

2 MAP P156, E3

Reservations are required for tours of this historic island monastery, tours are conducted by its multilingual Armenian monks, who amply demonstrate the institution's reputation for scholarship. The St Lazarus Monastery is a fascinating repository of Armenian history, art and culture – and much more besides. Significant manuscripts from its 170,000-item library are on display, alongside curios from Ancient Egypt, Rome, Sumeria and India. (https://mechitar.org/en)

Borges Labyrinth

DON MAMMOSER/SHUTTERSTOCK ©

Vittorio and Giorgio Cini

The father of Giorgio Cini, Vittorio, was an industrialist, appointed Minister of Communications by Mussolini in 1943. He resigned after six months as he disagreed with the war, and was later arrested by the Germans and imprisoned in Dachau concentration camp. His eldest son, Giorgio, managed to bribe guards to secure his release, whereupon he escaped to Switzerland. In 1949, Giorgio died in an air crash, and Vittorio set up Fondazione Giorgio Cini (p157) on the island of San Giorgio in his name.

Chiesa del Santissimo Redentore

CHURCH

3 MAP P156, C2

Built on Giudecca's waterfront to celebrate the city's deliverance from the Black Death, Palladio's Il Redentore was completed under Antonio da Ponte (of Rialto Bridge fame) in 1592. The theme is taken up in Paolo Piazza's monochrome *Venice's Offering for Liberation from the Plague of 1575–77* (1619), placed high above the entrance. Look for Tintoretto's *The Flagellation of Christ* (1588) on the third altar to the right. (www.chorusvenezia.org)

Casa dei Tre Oci

GALLERY

4 MAP P156, C2

On Giudecca's waterfront, the fanciful neo-Gothic 'House of Three Eyes' was built in 1913 by artist and photographer Mario de Maria, who conceived its distinctive brick facade with its three arched windows, from which the name comes. It now houses his photographic archive and exhibitions of contemporary art, especially photography. (www.treoci.org)

Acquolina Cooking School

COOKING

5 MAP P156, E3

These intimate cookery classes are held by Marika Contaldo in her flower-festooned Lido villa. Learn to make *cicheti* and taste wine, or take a half- or full-day course, the latter including a morning trip to the Rialto Market. The boat to the villa is included in the price. (www.acquolina.com)

Eating

La Palanca

VENETIAN €€

6 MAP P156, B2

Locals of all ages pour into this friendly Giudecca bar for *cicheti*, coffee and a *spritz*. However, it's at lunchtime that it really comes into its own. Nab a waterside seat with fabulous views of Venice to eat surprisingly sophisticated dishes, such as swordfish carpaccio with orange zest, alongside more rustic cuisine, like the delicious *pasta e fagioli* (pasta and bean soup). (www.facebook.com/LaPalancaGiudecca)

Trattoria Altanella VENETIAN €€

7 MAP P156, C2

Founded by fisherfolk in 1920 and still run by the same family, this wood-lined Giudecca trattoria is a wonderfully authentic place in a great position. With a flower-framed balcony overlooking the Canale della Giudecca, it serves classic Venetian fare such as potato gnocchi with cuttlefish, stuffed squid, and perfectly grilled John Dory (their great-grandfather's recipe) and anglerfish (their grandmother's recipe). The vintage interior is hung with paintings, reflecting the restaurant's popularity with local artists.

Trattoria ai Cacciatori VENETIAN €€

8 MAP P156, C2

If you hadn't guessed from the oversized gun hanging from the ceiling beams, this Giudecca restaurant is named for the hunters who once bagged lagoon waterfowl. Dishes are hearty but sophisticated, including both game and local seafood, and there are also waterfront seating for sunny days and views across to Venice.

Favorita VENETIAN €€€

9 MAP P156, F2

The family-run Favorita has been delivering slow, lazy lunches, bottles of fine wine and impeccable service since 1955. The menu is full of traditional Venetian seafood dishes such as *rombo* (turbot) simmered with cherry tomatoes and olives, crab *gnochetti* (mini-gnocchi) and classic fish risotto.

Boating on the Lagoon

Terra e Acqua (www.terraeacqua.com) offers wild rides to the outer edges of the lagoon on a sturdy motorised *bragozzo* (flat-bottomed fishing vessel) that accommodates up to 12 people. You can visit remote, abandoned quarantine islands, scud past salt marshes and see the hard-to-reach friary on Isola di San Francesco del Deserto. You can also hire beautifully kitted out electric boats from **Classic Boats Venice** (www.classicboatsvenice.com), based on La Certosa.

Venice Kayak (Map p156, F1; www.venicekayak.com) organises well-planned tours in the warren of Venice's canals and out to remote islands in the broad garden of the lagoon.

Magiche Voglie GELATO €

10 MAP P156, E3

Under a candy-striped awning, this family-owned gelateria serves the best gelato on the Lido, with unique flavours such as açai berry and caja fruit, or you can plump for the classic purplish-black cherry or Sicilian pistachio.

Drinking

Skyline

ROOFTOP BAR

11 MAP P156, B1

On Giudecca, with big, thrilling views over Venice and the lagoon, this rooftop bar attracts everyone from white-sneaker cruise passengers to the €300-sunglasses set. There are DJs on Sunday nights, and other occasional events can be checked on their website. (www.skylinebarvenice.it)

Hotel Villa Laguna

BAR

12 MAP P156, E3

Catch the sunset from the Lido on the terrace of the Habsburg-era Villa Laguna, with views over San Marco framed by a blushing pink sky. While this is essentially a restaurant, it also caters to crowds flocking for *aperitivi* (pre-dinner drinks). And it's very handy to get the Lido SME ferry terminal from here. (http://hotelvillalaguna.com)

Shopping

Cartavenezia

ARTS & CRAFTS

This, in a workshop (see 13 Map p156, B2) within Artisti Artigiani del Chiostro, is paper as you've never seen it before. Paper maestro Fernando di Masone embosses and sculpts handmade cotton paper into seamless raw-edged lampshades, hand-bound sketchbooks and paper versions of marble friezes that would seem equally at home in a Greek temple as in a modern loft. Use white gloves for easy, worry-free browsing. Paper-

Casa dei Tre Oci (p158)

VLADIMIR KOROSTYSHEVSKIY/SHUTTERSTOCK ©

sculpting courses are available by prior request. (www.cartavenezia.it)

Stefano Morasso GLASS

This small Giudecca workshop (see 13 Map p156, B2) is part of Artisti Artigiani del Chiostro. Stefano Morasso, who learned glassmaking in his father's studio on Murano, produces beautiful, work-of-art glasses and jewellery, assisted by his wife and son. You can see them at work in the studio as you browse the collection.

Artisti Artigiani del Chiostro ARTS & CRAFTS

13 MAP P156, B2

Dating from the 15th century, the cloister of the former Convent of St Cosmas and St Damian, on Giudecca, has been repurposed as a base for independent artisans to ply their craft, with open workshops including those of Cartavenezia and Stefano Morasso.

Fortuny Tessuti Artistici HOMEWARES

14 MAP P156, B1

Marcel Proust once bribed his mistress to stay with him by offering her a gown made from Fortuny fabric, and you can visit the hallowed showroom (appointments are preferred) at the secretive historic factory to browse upholstery fabrics or buy cushions. See even more fabrics at Museo Fortuny (p54) in San Marco. (www.fortuny.com)

A Spa with a View

On a 16-hectare private island, 20 minutes from Piazza San Marco, JW Marriott's Venetian **hotel** (Map p156, B4; www.jwvenice.com) feels very A-list. Matteo Thun's contemporary, minimalist interiors and rooms are elegant in the extreme, but it's the **rooftop spa and pools** (indoor and outdoor), with their four-poster loungers and unimpeded views across the lagoon, that really steal the show.

Non-hotel guests can access the island via the free shuttle from San Marco Giardinetti. Even the basic package that offers use of the facilities is worth the trip, or make a reservation for the Michelin-starred restaurant.

Explore

Murano, Burano & the Northern Islands

The islands to the north of Venice include Murano, a glassmaking nirvana; fishing village Burano, a centre for lace with houses painted brilliant hues decided by the government; and Torcello, with its huge Byzantine basilica on a near-deserted island, where Hemingway escaped from Venice to stay at the still-going Cipriani and write his worst novel, Across the River and Into the Trees.

The Short List

- ***Basilica di Santa Maria Assunta (p164)*** *Engaging with angelic visions and demonic depictions at the lagoon's oldest church on Torcello.*
- ***Museo del Vetro (p167)*** *Seeing incredible glass-blowing artisanship on the island of Murano.*
- ***Discover Burano*** *Wandering the streets of the picturesque village that's all the colours of the rainbow.*

Getting There & Around

Vaporetto Murano: lines 3, 4.1 and 4.2, lines 12 and 13 stop only at Faro; Burano, Mazzorbo and Torcello: line 12 from Fondamente Nove or Murano-Faro stop; line 9 from Burano also heads to Torcello; Le Vignole and Sant'Erasmo: line 13 from Fondamente Nove via Murano-Faro.

Murano, Burano & the Northern Islands Map on p168

Burano OLGA GAVRILOVA/SHUTTERSTOCK ©

Top Experience

Gaze at Byzantine Splendour in Torcello

MAP P168, D2

https://itorcello.it

Torcello's population ebbed away as Venice grew (fewer than 20 people live here today). The 7th-century basilica of Santa Maria Assunta has remained, as if preserved in aspic, neither remodelled nor changed. Its extraordinary Byzantine mosaics show the Eastern influence of the city's contact with Constantinople.

Madonna & Last Judgement Mosaics

The restrained brick exterior betrays no hint of the gilded scene that unfolds within, all the more striking set against the plain walls of the rest of the church. In the 12th-century apse mosaic, the Madonna (pictured) rises in the east, a dominant figure, like the sun above a field of Torcello poppies. The back wall bears an extraordinary and complex Last Judgement mosaic that shows the Adriatic as a sea nymph ushering souls lost at sea towards St Peter, while a devil tips the scales of justice and the Antichrist's minions drag sinners into hell.

Chapel Mosaics & Other Key Works

The right-hand chapel is capped with another 12th-century mosaic showing Christ flanked by angels and Sts Augustine, Ambrose, Martin and Gregory amid symbolic plants: lilies (representing purity), wheat and grapes (representing the bread and wine of the Eucharist) and poppies (evoking Torcello's island setting).

The polychrome marble floor is another medieval masterpiece, with swirling designs and interlocking wheels symbolising eternal life. Saints line up atop the iconostasis, their gravity foiled by a Byzantine screen teeming with peacocks, rabbits and other fanciful beasts.

Museo di Torcello

Relics of Torcello's 7th- to 11th-century Byzantine empire are shown inside 13th-century Palazzo del Consiglio, home to the **Museo di Torcello** (https://servizimetropolitani.ve.it/en/torcello-museum/the-museum). Mosaic fragments show the mastery achieved in Torcello, while upstairs archives contain Graeco-Roman artefacts from the lost civilisation of Altinum.

★ Top Tips

- Climb the *campanile* (bell tower) for a heavenly view over the swampy islands and get a fascinating insight into how Venice itself must have once looked.
- Various combo tickets are offered, including the church, *campanile*, audio guide and the neighbouring museum.
- To get under the skin of Torcello, stay here overnight.

Take a Break

Locanda Cipriani (p170), where Hemingway stayed to write, offers bellinis and excellent pasta in a splendid rose garden. Otherwise, hop aboard the *vaporetto* to Mazzorbo for lagoon-inspired fare in the vineyard of Venissa Osteria (p170), an upmarket *osteria* (casual tavern) with rooms.

Walking Tour

Art of Glass in Murano

Unrivalled masters of glass art since the 10th century, Venice's glass artisans moved to Murano in the 13th century to contain fornace *(furnace) fire hazards. Trade secrets were so closely guarded that glass masters who left the city were threatened with assassination. See the unparalleled work along Murano's picturesque main drags; this is the best place to buy glassware direct from the producer and avoid cheap replicas.*

Walk Facts

Start Basilica dei SS Maria e Donato; *vaporetto* Museo

Finish Marina e Susanna Sent Studio; *vaporetto* Colonna

Length 1.5km; 45 minutes

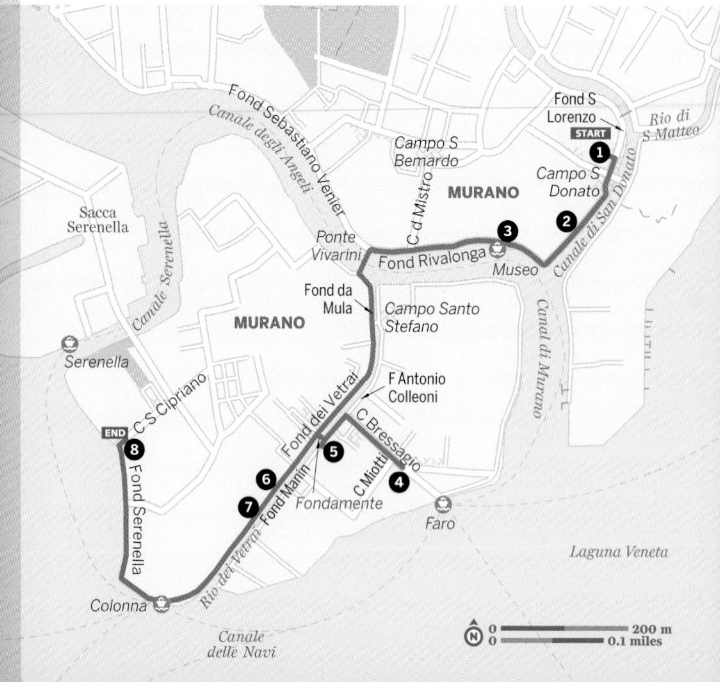

❶ Basilica dei SS Maria e Donato

Fire-breathing is the unifying theme of Murano's medieval **Basilica dei SS Maria e Donato**, with its astounding 12th-century gilded-glass apse mosaic of the Madonna made in Murano's *fornaci* (furnaces) and the bones of a dragon, apparently slain by St Donatus of Arezzo, hanging behind the altar. Underfoot is a Byzantine-style 12th-century mosaic patterned pavement of griffons, eagles and peacocks rendered in precious stones.

❷ Museo del Vetro

Since 1861, Murano's glassmaking prowess has been celebrated at the **Museo del Vetro** (www.museovetro.visitmuve.it) in Gothic Palazzo Giustinian, and its eight rooms have curated displays of objects dating from the 5th century BCE to the present day, with delicate glassware created using otherworldly skills.

❸ Davide Penso

The work of **Davide Penso** is like nothing else on the island: in his seaweed glassware, fronds of glass flow to capture a sense of moving water, and his shop also has necklaces formed from opaque glass discs. His glassware has been exhibited at the Guggenheim and various glass museums from Russia to Japan.

❹ Tagliapietra

On the way to the Faro *vaporetto* stop, look in through the doors of **Tagliapietra** and see its open workshop and the glassblowers in action, moulding molten glass fresh from the furnace.

❺ ElleElle

Nason Moretti has made modernist magic in glass since the 1950s, and the colourful glassware at **ElleElle** (https://elleellemurano.com) still has a sleek mid-century style.

❻ Venini

Of the big houses, **Venini** remains the most relevant, defining modernist trends since the 1930s. Even if you can't afford the price tag, pop in to see glass by design greats like Carlo Scarpa and Fabio Novembre, who created giant 'Happy Pills' made from glass.

❼ Cesare Toffolo

Incredibly elaborate glassware is the signature here, with gold-leafed winged goblets and mind-boggling miniatures by legendary master glass-blower **Cesare Toffolo**.

❽ Marina e Susanna Sent Studio

The Sent sisters are fourth-generation glassmakers, and you can see their strikingly contemporary work at **Marina e Susanna Sent Studio**, including ice-blue glass waterfall necklaces and lava-red beads on paper collars. Ask to open jewellery drawers to browse hidden treasures.

A B C D

1 2 3 4 5 6

Palude della Rosa

Basilica di Santa Maria Assunta

Torcello

3

Palude del Monte

Canale Borgognoni

Palude dei Laghi

Isola Buel del Lovo

Venissa Ristorante

5

Canale di Burano

Mazzorbo

Burano

7

4

2

Museo del Merletto

Isola Carbonera

LAGUNA VENETA

Isola della Madonna del Monte

Isola di San Francesco del Deserto

Isola di Tessera

Isola di San Giacomo in Palude

Murano

8

Isola del Lazzaretto Nuovo

6

Sant'Erasmo

Cimitero di San Michele

1

Isola di San Michele

Le Vignole

Canale di Treporti

0 2 km
0 1 miles

Punta Sabbioni

For reviews see

Top Experiences	p165
Sights	p169
Eating	p170
Drinking	p171
Shopping	p171

Lido di Venezia

Porto del Lido

Golfo di Venezia

A B C D

Sights

Cimitero di San Michele

CEMETERY

1 MAP P168, A5

Until Napoleon established a city cemetery on this little island, Venetians had been buried in parish plots across town – not an ideal solution in a watery city. Today, it's a serene spot, with the graves punctuated by cypress trees. It is the final resting place for Ezra Pound, Joseph Brodsky, Sergei Diaghilev and Igor Stravinsky. Venetians are still buried here, but each plot is only leased for around a decade, after which the bones are transferred to make space for new burials. David Chipperfield Architects added a minimalist basalt-clad extension in the early 2000s.

Museo del Merletto

MUSEUM

2 MAP P168, D3

On the main square of Burano, the Lace Museum tells the story of a craft that cut across social boundaries, endured for centuries and evoked the epitome of sophistication reached during the Republic's heyday. Lacemaking was both a creative expression and a highly lucrative craft, although the skill was nearly lost several times as handmade lace went in and out of fashion. (www.museomerletto.visitmuve.it)

Cimitero di San Michele

Regatta Revelry

The biggest event in the northern lagoon calendar is in May, with the **Vogalonga long row** (www.vogalonga.com) from Venice to Murano and back. A show of endurance, this 32km 'long row' starts with over 1500 boats launching outside the Palazzo Ducale; it then loops past Burano and Murano and ends at Punta della Dogana with cheers, sweat and enough prosecco to numb any blisters. Plan in advance and find a grassy picnic spot on Mazzorbo. If you'd like to have a go yourself, get in touch with Row Venice (p130).

Eating

Locanda Cipriani VENETIAN €€€

3 MAP P168, D2

On Torcello, and run by the Cipriani family since 1935, the Locanda's guest rooms are where Hemingway escaped to write in the 1950s. The wood-beamed dining room opens on to a rose garden, and staff buzz about in dapper bow ties, theatrically silver-serving every dish. The kitchen is just as precise, delivering pillowy gnocchi, perfectly cooked fish and decadent chocolate mousse. (www.locandacipriani.com)

Trattoria al Gatto Nero VENETIAN €€€

4 MAP P168, D3

On Burano, you'll need to book ahead at Trattoria al Gatto Nero, especially for canalside seating. Once there, tuck into homemade *tagliolini* (ribbon pasta) with spider crab, whole grilled fish and perfect house-baked biscuits. (www.gattonero.com)

Venissa Osteria VENETIAN €€

5 MAP P168, D2

A more affordable companion piece to its Michelin-starred sister, this upmarket *osteria* (casual tavern) offers updates on Venetian classics such as marinated fish, duck tagliatelle and *bigoli in salsa* (thick wholemeal pasta with anchovies). For an extra treat, splash out on a glass of dorona, the prestigious golden-hued wine varietal only grown here. (www.venissa.it)

Acquastanca VENETIAN €€

6 MAP P168, A4

This little Murano restaurant is the best choice in the town of glass, adorned with antique Murano mirrors, wooden fish and wow-factor Murano sculpture. Seafood features prominently on a menu that includes octopus with chickpeas and a panoply of pasta. (www.acquastanca.it)

Venissa: A Mazzorbo Renaissance

In 1999, Gianluca Bisol, a prosecco producer from Valdobbiadene, heard of an ancient vineyard enclosed by medieval walls on Mazzorbo. He rented the land from the city and set about rehabilitating the rare Renaissance dorona grape from the surviving 88 vines.

He later converted the farm buildings into a contemporary six-room **guesthouse** and **Venissa Osteria**, before adding a Michelin-starred (and Michelin-green-starred for its eco-credentials) garden **restaurant** (Map p168, D2; www.venissa.it).

The entire Mazzorbo operation is now managed by Gianluca's son Matteo, who has also opened lovely **Casa Burano** (www.casaburano.it), an *albergo diffuso* (multi-venue hotel) with 13 rooms spread through five cottages on Burano.

Drinking

Caffè-Bar Palmisano — CAFE

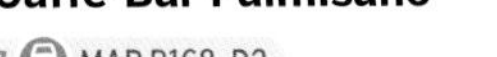

7 MAP P168, D2

Refuel with espresso at this cafe's sun-shaded pavement tables and return later to celebrate photo-safari triumphs over *spritz* or wine with regular crowds of fisherfolk and university students.

Shopping

Emilia — ARTS & CRAFTS

The fourth generation of the family of Emilia di Ammendola is continuing their lacemaking tradition in this flagship store (see 2 Map p168, D3); there's another on Calle San Mauro and a branch in Los Angeles. Prices befit the quality (ie out of this world). There's also a small family museum upstairs. (www.emiliaburano.it)

Fornace Mian — GLASS

8 MAP P168, A4

Shuffle past the typical Murano kitsch (glass pandas, parrots in trees etc) and you'll find one of the best ranges of classic stemware on the island. If there isn't enough of your favourite design in stock, it can be made to order and shipped internationally. (www.fornacemian.com)

Survival Guide

Canal in Castello (p135) ABIGAIL BLASI ©

Before You Go

Book Your Stay

- Book ahead for weekend getaways and high-season visits.
- Although Venice is a small city, getting around it can be complicated, so carefully plan where you stay. Easy access to a *vaporetto* (small passenger ferry) stop is key.
- Check individual hotel websites for online deals.
- Confirm arrival at least 72 hours in advance, or hotels may assume you've changed plans.
- For low-season savings of 40% or more, plan visits for November, early December or January to March (except Carnevale). Deals may be found July and August.

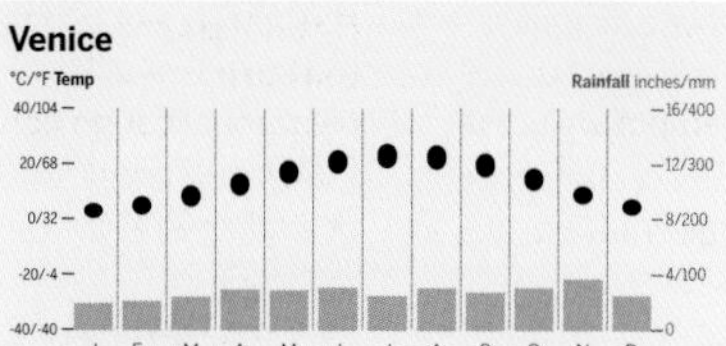

When to Go

- **Spring (Mar–May)** Damp but lovely as ever indoors. Bring an umbrella and enjoy bargain rates – except at Easter.
- **Summer (Jun–Aug)** The Biennale draws the crowds. Temperatures rise and the Rialto is hot, crowded and expensive. Locals escape to the Lido.
- **Autumn (Sep–Nov)** After the Venice Film Festival and the Biennale, crowds retreat and rates drop, but the sun still shines.
- **Winter (Dec–Feb)** Chilly days with some fog, but nights are sociable, especially during Carnevale.

Useful Websites

Luxrest Venice (www.luxrest-venice.com) Carefully curated, hand-picked selection of apartments.

Lonely Planet (lonelyplanet.com/italy/venice/hotels) Expert author reviews of the city's best accommodation.

Venice Prestige (www.veniceprestige.com) Venetian apartments to rent in aristocratic palaces in the best locations in town.

Views on Venice (www.viewsonvenice.com) Apartments picked for their personality, character and view, of course.

Fairbnb Venice (https://fairbnb.coop) A community-powered home-sharing platform where 50% of booking fees support local projects.

Best Budget

Allo Squero (www.allosquero.it) Cannaregio home comforts.

Le Terese (www.leterese.com) A stylish architect-styled room and apartment.

Albergo San Samuele (www.hotelsansamuele.com) Rock-bottom prices right by Palazzo Grassi.

Generator (www.generatorhostels.com) Contemporary hostel cool with canal views.

Combo Venezia (www.thisiscombo.com/location/venezia/) Plain rooms in a former convent turned hostel with a buzzy cafe.

Best Midrange

Oltre Il Giardino (www.oltreilgiardino-venezia.com) A romantic garden retreat, once home to Alma Mahler's widow.

Residenza de L'Osmarin (www.residenzadelosmarin.com) A true B&B with quilted bedspreads and a slap-up breakfast.

Casa Burano (www.casaburano.it) Pastel-coloured cottages full of locally crafted furnishings.

Best Top End

Gritti Palace (www.thegrittipalace.com) Grand Canal rooms in a stunning doge's palace.

Al Ponte Antico (www.alponteantico.com) Old-world glamour accompanied by gracious service.

Hotel Palazzo Barbarigo (www.palazzobarbarigo.com) Seductive rooms handily supplied with fainting couches.

Palazzo Abadessa (www.abadessa.com) Frescoed rooms, canal views and a lily-scented garden.

Arriving in Venice

Stazione Venezia Santa Lucia

All mainland trains terminate in Venice's **Santa Lucia train station** (www.veneziasantalucia.it), appearing on signs within Venice as Ferrovia. The station has a helpful **tourist office** (www.veneziaunica.it) opposite platform 3 where you can obtain a map and buy *vaporetto* tickets, and a **left-luggage depot** opposite platform 1.

Vaporetto

Vaporetti connect Santa Lucia train station with all parts of Venice. Lines include the following:

Line 1 Covers the Grand Canal to San Marco and the Lido every 10 minutes.

Line 2 Covers the Grand Canal with fewer stops, returning via Giudecca.

Lines 4.1 & 4.2 Circles Venice's outer perimeter. Convenient for Cannaregio and Castello.

Lines 5.1 & 5.2 Covers the 4.1 and 4.2 route, plus the Lido, with fewer stops.

Line N All-night service that stops along Giudecca, the Grand Canal, San Marco and the Lido.

Water Taxi

The water taxi stand is outside the train station on Fondamente Cossetti; fares start at €15 and add up quickly at €2 per minute.

Marco Polo Airport

Marco Polo Airport (www.veniceairport.it) is Venice's main international airport and is located in Tessera, 12km east of Mestre.

Inside the terminal you'll find ticket offices for water taxis and Alilaguna water bus transfers, an ATM, currency exchange offices, a **left-luggage office** and a Vènezia Unica tourist office (p182) where you can pick up pre-ordered travel cards and a map.

Alilaguna Airport Shuttle

Alilaguna (www.alilaguna.it) operates four water shuttles that link the airport with various parts of Venice at a cost of €8 to Murano and €15 to all other landing stages. The ride takes 45 to 90 minutes to reach most destinations. Lines include the following:

Linea Blu (Blue Line) Stops at Lido, San Marco and Dorsoduro.

Linea Rossa (Red Line) Stops at Murano and Lido.

Linea Arancia (Orange Line) Stops at Stazione Venezia Santa Lucia, Rialto and San Marco via the Grand Canal.

Linea Gialla (Yellow Line) Stops at Murano and Fondamente Nove (Cannaregio).

Bus

Piazzale Roma is the only point within central Venice accessible by bus. *Vaporetto* lines and water taxis depart from Piazzale Roma docks.

ACTV (http://actv.avmspa.it/en) Bus 5 runs between Marco Polo Airport and Piazzale Roma (€10, 30 minutes, four per hour).

ATVO (www.atvo.it/en-venice-airport.html) Buses depart from the airport to **Piazzale Roma** (€10, 25 minutes, every 30 minutes from 8am to midnight).

Water Taxi

- Water taxis can be booked at the **Consorzio Motoscafi Venezia** (www.motoscafivenezia.it) or **Venezia Taxi** (www.veneziataxi.it) desks in the arrivals hall, or directly at the dock. Private taxis cost from €110 for up to four passengers and all their luggage.
- A shared taxi costs from €25 per person with a €6 surcharge for night-time arrivals. Seats should be booked online at www.venicelink.com. Be aware that shared taxis can wait some time to fill up and have set drop-off points in Venice.
- Boats seat a maximum of 10 people and accommodate up to 10 bags.

Taxi

A taxi from the aiport to Piazzale Roma costs €50. From there you can either hop on a *vaporetto* or pick up a **water taxi** at Fondamente Cossetti.

Car

- Cars cannot be taken into central Venice. At Piazzale Roma and Tronchetto parking garages expect to pay from €15 per day.
- From Piazzale Roma docks, you can take a *vaporetto* or water taxi.
- A **monorail** (www.avmspa.it), also known as the People Mover, connects the Tronchetto parking lots to Piazzale Roma (€1.50 per person).

Getting Around

Vaporetto

- The city's main mode of public transport is the *vaporetto*.
- **ACTV** (http://actv.avmspa.it/en) runs all public transport in Venice, including all waterborne public transport.
- Major stops often have two separate docks serving the same *vaporetto* line, heading in opposite directions. Check landing dock signs to make sure you're at the right dock for the direction you want.
- Main lines get full fast, especially between 8am and 10am and between 6pm and 8pm. Also, boats can be overcrowded during Carnevale and in peak season.
- Line N offers all-night local service covering Giudecca, the Grand Canal, San Marco and the Lido (11.30pm to 4am, about every 40 minutes).
- Inter-island ferry services to Murano, Torcello, the Lido and other lagoon islands are usually provided on larger *motonave* (big inter-island *vaporetti*).

Tickets & Passes

- Vènezia Unica (p182) is the main ticket seller, and you can purchase *vaporetto* tickets at booths at most landing stations. Tickets and multiday passes can also be pre-purchased online.
- A one-way ticket costs €9.50.
- If you're going to be using the *vaporetto* frequently (more than three trips), consider a Travel Card, which allows unlimited travel in set time periods (one-/two-/three-/seven-day passes cost €25/35/45/65).
- Always validate your ticket at yellow dockside machines at first usage. If you're caught without a valid ticket you'll be fined €59 (plus the €9.50 fare) on the spot.
- People aged six to 29 holding a Rolling Venice card (p180; €6) can get a three-day ticket for €27 (instead of €45) at tourist offices.

Gondola

- Rates are €80 for 40 minutes (€100 for 35 minutes from 7pm to 8am), not including songs or tips. Additional time is charged in 20-minute increments (day/night €40/50).
- Gondolas cluster at *stazi* (stops) along the Grand Canal and near major monuments and tourist hot spots, but you can also book a pick-up by calling **Ente Gondola** (www.gondolavenezia.it).

Traghetto

A *traghetto* is a cash-only gondola service that local workers use to cross the Grand Canal between bridges (€2, 9am to 6pm, some routes to noon). There are seven crossings on the Canal: just look for Traghetto signs.

Water Taxi

- Licensed water taxis offer stylish transport in sleek teak boats.
- Fares start at €15 plus €2 per minute, €5 extra if they're called to your hotel. There's a €10 surcharge for night trips

(10pm to 6am), a €5 surcharge for additional luggage (above five pieces) and a €10 surcharge for each extra passenger above the first four. Tipping isn't required.

- If you order a water taxi through your hotel or a travel agent, you will be subject to a surcharge.
- Even if you're in a hurry, don't encourage your taxi driver to speed – *motoschiaffi* (motorboat wakes) expose Venice's ancient foundations to degradation.

Bicycle

- Cycling is banned in central Venice.
- On the Lido, cycling is a pleasant way to reach distant beaches.
- **Lido on Bike** (Map p156, E3; www.lidoonbike.it) is near the *vaporetto* stop; ID is needed for rental.

Essential Information

Accessible Travel

With nearly 400 footbridges and endless stairs, Venice is not an easy place for travellers with disabilities.

- *Vaporetti* are the most effective way to access sites and avoid bridges. Passengers in wheelchairs travel for just €1.50, while their companion travels free.
- The most accessible tourist office is the one off Piazza San Marco.
- With ID, most museums offer free or discounted admission to disabled visitors with one companion.
- A printable *Accessible Venice* map is available from the tourist office. The map marks out the area around each water-bus stop that can be accessed without crossing a bridge. In addition, the website provides 12 'barrier-free' itineraries, which can be downloaded.
- Of the other islands, Murano, Burano, the Lido and Torcello are all fairly easy to access.

Organisations

L'Altra Venezia (www.laltravenezia.it) Offers half- and full-day city and lagoon tours in specially adapted boats that can accommodate up to seven people (maximum four wheelchairs). Tours can be 'pilot only' or with a guide, and include lunch on-board or in local restaurants.

Rome & Italy (www.romeanditaly.com/accessible) A mainstream travel agency with an accessible tourism arm that offers two half-day customised tours in Venice to the Doge's palace and Torcello island, accessible accommodation, and equipment and vehicle hire.

Accessible Italy (www.accessibleitaly.com) A San Marino–based nonprofit company that specialises in holiday services for people with disabilities, including equipment rental, adapted vehicle hire and arranging personal assistants. In Venice, it offers multiday individual, group and bespoke tours.

Sage Traveling (www.sagetraveling.com) A US-based accessible-travel agency, offering tailor-made tours in Europe. Check out its website for a detailed access guide to Venice, which includes tips on how to use the *vaporetto* and water taxis, accessible walking and boating tours, and hotels.

Business Hours

The hours listed here are a general guide; individual establishments can vary.

Banks 8.30am to 1.30pm and 3.30pm to 5.30pm Monday to Friday; some open Saturday mornings.

Restaurants Noon to 2.30pm and 7pm to 10pm.

Shops 10am to 1pm and 3.30pm to 7pm (or 4pm to 7.30pm) Monday to Saturday.

Discount Cards

The tourist information portal, **Vènezia Unica** (p182), brings together a range of discount passes and services, and enables you to tailor them to your needs and pre-purchase online. Services and passes on offer include the following:

- land and water transfers to the airport and cruise terminal
- ACTV Travel Cards
- museum and church passes
- select parking
- citywide wi-fi
- prepaid access to public toilets.

If purchasing online, you need to print out your voucher displaying your reservation number (PNR) and carry it with you, then simply present it at the various attractions for admission/access.

To use public transport, you will need to obtain a free card (you will need your PNR code to do this), which is then 'loaded' with credit. Get this at the ACTV ticket machines at Marco Polo Airport, ticket desks at *vaporetto* stops and Vènezia Unica offices.

Chorus Pass

Offers single entry to 16 churches (adult/student under 29 years €12/8). Valid for one year. Buy at participating churches or online at Vènezia Unica.

Civic Museum Pass

This pass (adult/reduced €41/23) is valid for six months and covers single entry to 11 civic museums, including Palazzo Ducale and the Museo Correr. Available from any civic museum, at the tourist office or online at Vènezia Unica.

City Pass

City passes are available from Vènezia Unica. The most useful:

City Pass (adult/junior €52.90/31.90) Valid for seven days, offering entrance to 11 civic museums, 16 Chorus churches, the Fondazione Querini Stampalia and the Museo Ebraico (Jewish Museum). It also includes free admission to the casino.

St Mark's City Pass (€38.90/30.40) A reduced version of the City Pass allowing entry to the three civic museums on Piazza San Marco, plus three churches on the Chorus Circuit and the Fondazione Querini Stampalia.

Other Combined Museum Tickets

- A combined ticket to Ca' d'Oro and Palazzo Grimani costs €17/10/free for an adult/student/senior and is valid for three months.

- A combined ticket to the Palazzo Grassi and Punta della Dogana costs €15/12 (adult/ reduced).

Rolling Venice Card

Visitors aged 6 to 29 years should pick up the €6 Rolling Venice card (from tourist offices and most ACTV public transport ticket points), entitling purchase of a 72-hour public transport pass (€27) and discounts on airport transfers, museums, monuments and cultural events.

Electricity

Type F
230V/50Hz

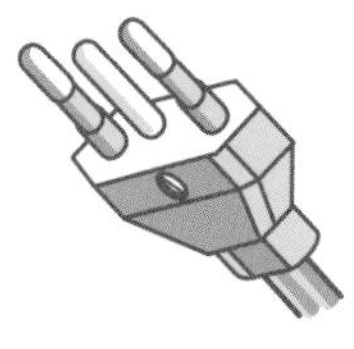

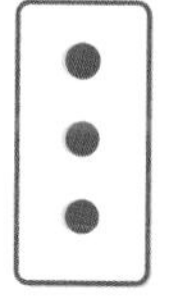

Type L
220V/50Hz

Money

ATMs Widely available. It's handy to have some cash in Venice.

Credit cards Accepted at almost all hotels, B&Bs and shops.

Money changers At banks, airport and some hotels; you'll need ID.

Tipping Ten per cent optional for good restaurant, hotel and gondola services.

Public Holidays

Holidays that may affect opening hours and transit schedules:

Capodanno/Anno Nuovo (New Year's Day) 1 January

Epifania/Befana (Epiphany) 6 January

Pasquetta/Lunedì dell'Angelo (Easter Monday) March/April

Giorno della Liberazione (Liberation Day) 25 April

Festa del Lavoro (Labour Day) 1 May

Festa della Repubblica (Republic Day) 2 June

Ferragosto (Feast of the Assumption) 15 August

Ognissanti (All Saints' Day) 1 November

Immaculata Concezione (Feast of the Immaculate Conception) 8 December

Natale (Christmas Day) 25 December

Festa di Santo Stefano (Boxing Day) 26 December

Safe Travel

Precautions Mind your step on slippery canal banks, especially after rains. Watch out for petty theft around Venice's train station.

Children Few canal banks and bridges have railings, and most Gothic palaces have lots of stairs.

Rising water Flooding in low-lying areas is a regular occurrence in Venice.

COVID-19 At the time of writing, under Italy's anti-COVID regulations, you're required to wear an FFP2 mask on all public transport including ferries. The rule is strictly enforced – you can't travel without a mask. Regulations can change at short notice – check the latest at www.italia.it/en/covid-19-italy-travel-guidelines.

Dos & Don'ts

- Do keep right along narrow lanes and let people pass on the left.
- Don't linger on small bridges taking photographs at lunchtime and 3pm during the school run. And avoid selfie sticks which threaten to poke passers-by in the eye.
- Don't picnic on the steps of bridges or churches.
- Do offer help to people struggling with strollers or bags on bridges.
- Don't push. Allow passengers to disembark before boarding boats. Pay attention to calls of *'Permesso!'* (Pardon!) as people try to exit busy boats.

Telephone Services

Mobile Phones

GSM and tri-band phones can be used in Italy with a local SIM card.

Phone Codes

Italy's country code is 39. The city code for Venice is 041. The city code is an integral part of the number and must always be dialled. Toll-free (free-phone) numbers are known as *numeri verdi* and usually start with 800.

International Calls

The cheapest options for calling internationally are free or low-cost computer programs such as Skype, FaceTime and Viber, cut-rate call centres or international dialling cards, which are sold at newsstands and tobacconists.

If you're calling an international number from an Italian phone, you must dial 00 to get an international line, then the relevant country and city codes, followed by the telephone number.

To call Venice from abroad, call the international access number for Italy (011 in the United States, 00 from most other countries), Italy's country code 39, then the Venice area code 041, followed by the telephone number.

Toilets

Public toilets Available near tourist attractions (€1.50); open from 7am to 7pm.

Bars and cafes Strictly for customers only. Look before you sit: even in women's bathrooms, some toilets don't have seats.

Museums This is your best option – where available.

Tourist Information

Vènezia Unica (www.veneziaunica.it) runs all tourist information services and offices in Venice. It provides information on sights, itineraries, day trips, transport, special events, shows and temporary exhibitions. Discount passes can be prebooked on its website. Find offices at Marco Polo Airport, Santa Lucia train station and on Piazza San Marco.

Visas

Not required for EU citizens. Nationals of Australia, Brazil, Canada, Japan, New Zealand, the UK and the USA do not need visas for visits of up to 90 days. For more information, visit the Italian foreign ministry website (www.esteri.it).

Language

Regional dialects are an important part of identity in many parts of Italy, but you'll have no trouble being understood in Venice or anywhere else in the country if you stick to standard Italian, which is what we've used in this chapter.

The sounds used in Italian can all be found in English. If you read our pronunciation guides as if they were English, you'll be understood. The stressed syllables are indicated with italics. Note that *ai* is pronounced as in 'aisle', *ay* as in 'say', *ow* as in 'how', *dz* as the 'ds' in 'lids', and that *r* is a strong and rolled sound.

To enhance your trip with a phrasebook, visit lonelyplanet.com.

Basics

Hello.
Buongiorno. bwon·*jor*·no

Goodbye.
Arrivederci. a·ree·ve·*der*·chee

How are you?
Come sta? *ko*·me sta

Fine. And you?
Bene. E Lei? *be*·ne e lay

Please.
Per favore. per fa·*vo*·re

Thank you.
Grazie. *gra*·tsye

Excuse me.
Mi scusi. mee *skoo*·zee

Sorry.
Mi dispiace. mee dees·*pya*·che

Yes./No.
Sì./No. see/no

I don't understand.
Non capisco. non ka·*pee*·sko

Do you speak English?
Parla inglese? *par*·la een·*gle*·ze

Eating & Drinking

I'd like ...	*Vorrei ...*	vo·*ray* ..
a coffee	*un caffè*	oon ka·*fe*
a table	*un tavolo*	oon *ta*·vo·lo
the menu	*il menù*	eel me·*noo*
two beers	*due birre*	doo·e *bee*·re

What would you recommend?
Cosa mi consiglia? ko·za mee kon·see·lya

Enjoy the meal!
Buon appetito! bwon a·pe·*tee*·to

That was delicious!
Era squisito! e·ra skwee·zee·to

Cheers!
Salute! sa·*loo*·te

Please bring the bill.
Mi porta il conto, per favore? mee *por*·ta eel *kon* to per fa·*vo*·re

Shopping

I'd like to buy ...
Vorrei comprare ... vo·*ray* kom·*pra*·re ...

I'm just looking.
Sto solo guardando. sto *so*·lo gwar·*dan*·do

How much is this?

Quanto costa questo?	kwan·to kos·ta kwe·sto

It's too expensive.

È troppo caro/ cara. (m/f)	e tro·po ka·ro/ ka·ra

Emergencies

Help!

Aiuto!	a·yoo·to

Call the police!

Chiami la polizia!	kya·mee la po·lee·tsee·a

Call a doctor!

Chiami un medico!	kya·mee oon me·dee·ko

I'm sick.

Mi sento male.	mee sen·to ma·le

I'm lost.

Mi sono perso/ persa. (m/f)	mee so·no per·so/ per·sa

Where are the toilets?

Dove sono i gabinetti?	do·ve so·no ee ga·bee·ne·tee

Time & Numbers

What time is it?

Che ora è?	ke o·ra e

It's (two) o'clock.

Sono le (due).	so·no le (doo·e)

morning	*mattina*	ma·tee·na
afternoon	*pomeriggio*	po·me·ree·jo
evening	*sera*	se·ra
yesterday	*ieri*	ye·ree
today	*oggi*	o·jee
tomorrow	*domani*	do·ma·nee

1	*uno*	oo·no
2	*due*	doo·e
3	*tre*	tre
4	*quattro*	kwa·tro
5	*cinque*	cheen·kwe
6	*sei*	say
7	*sette*	se·te
8	*otto*	o·to
9	*nove*	no·ve
10	*dieci*	dye·chee
100	*cento*	chen·to
1000	*mille*	mee·le

Transport & Directions

Where's ...?

Dov'è ...?	do·ve ...

What's the address?

Qual'è l'indirizzo?	kwa·le leen·dee·ree·tso

Can you show me (on the map)?

Può mostrarmi (sulla pianta)?	pwo mos·trar·mee (soo·la pyan·ta)

At what time does the ... leave?

A che ora parte ...?	a ke o·ra par·te

Does it stop at ...?

Si ferma a ...?	see fer·ma a ...

How do I get there?

Come ci si arriva?	ko·me chee see a·ree·va

bus	*l'autobus*	low·to·boos
ticket	*un biglietto*	oon bee·lye·to
timetable	*orario*	o·ra·ryo
train	*il treno*	eel tre·no

Behind the Scenes

Send Us Your Feedback

We love to hear from travellers – your comments help make our books better. We read every word, and we guarantee that your feedback goes straight to the authors. Visit **lonelyplanet.com/contact** to submit your updates and suggestions.

Note: We may edit, reproduce and incorporate your comments in Lonely Planet products such as guidebooks, websites and digital products, so let us know if you don't want your comments reproduced or your name acknowledged. For a copy of our privacy policy visit **lonelyplanet.com/legal**.

Helena Thanks

Thanks to Marina, Alessandro, Blanca and friends for their welcome and their insights, and to Maddalena for her invaluable help, including finding a piano. To Art for coming with me and making the trip even more wonderful, and to Angela and Grahame for my first trip to Venice.

Abigail Thanks

Many thanks to my co-author Helena, to Angela Tinson for commissioning me to cover this glorious place, and to the great Lonely Planet in-house team. *Tante grazie* to Jane da Mosto and the We are Venice team, to Giovanna Zanella for her great tips, and to Luca, Gabriel, Jack Roman and Vale for being the best Italian *famiglia*.

Acknowledgements

Cover photograph: (front) A canal in Murano. Yasonya/Shutterstock ©; (back) Carnevale masks. vuk8691/ Getty Images ©

Photographs pp34–5 (from left): Iakov Kalinin/Shutterstock ©, Eva Pruchova/Shutterstock ©, Perekotypole/Shutterstock ©

This Book

This 6th edition of Lonely Planet's *Pocket Venice* guidebook was researched and written by Helena Smith and Abigail Blasi. The previous edition was written by Paula Hardy, Peter Dragicevich and Duncan Garwood. This guidebook was produced by the following:

Commissioning Editor Angela Tinson

Product Editor Barbara Delissen

Book Designer Norma Brewer

Cartographer James Leversha

Coordinating Editor Andrea Dobbin

Assisting Editors Shauna Daly, Soo Hamilton

Cover Researcher Hannah Blackie

Thanks to Katie Connolly, Victoria Harrison, Jane da Mosto, Marina Dora Martino, Pierpaolo Pregnolato, Giovanna Zanella

Index

See also separate subindexes for:
Eating p188
Drinking p189
Entertainment p190
Shopping p190

Eating

Drinking

Entertainment

Shopping

Sights 000
Map Pages **000**

Our Writers

Helena Smith

Helena is a writer, photographer and videographer who was brought up in Scotland and Malawi. She creates original projects about community and eco travel, and co-runs a social enterprise creating space for nature in the city: wearewilder.co.uk.

Abigail Blasi

Abigail Blasi has lived in Hong Kong, Rome, Copenhagen and London. She is married to an Italian, and tries to spend as much time as possible in the Beautiful Country. She specialises in writing on Italy, Denmark, Malta and India, but her travel writing has taken her from Tobago to Tunisia, and from Mauritania to Margate. As well as writing for Lonely Planet, she contributes to the Telegraph, Times, the Independent, France Today, and more.

Published by Lonely Planet Global Limited
CRN 554153
6th edition – Apr 2023
ISBN 978 1 83869 617 7

10 9 8 7 6 5 4 3 2
Printed in Malaysia